THE GAMBLER'S
BIBLE

THE GAMBLER'S BIBLE

By
Margaret Cronin Fisk

DRAKE PUBLISHERS INC.
NEW YORK • LONDON

Published in 1976 by
DRAKE PUBLISHERS INC.
801 Second Ave.
New York, N.Y. 10017

Copyright 1976 by Margaret C. Fisk
All Rights Reserved.

ISBN: 0-8473-1027-2
LC: 75-13600

Printed in The United States of America

To Alan

CONTENTS

THE GAMBLER'S
BIBLE

Introduction

"Of all the human emotions none is so productive of evil and immorality as gambling." — Tallyrand

"The urge to gamble is so universal and its practice so pleasurable, that I assume it must be evil." —Heywood Broun

"Smart is better than lucky." —Titanic Thompson

Gambling—not oil, automobiles, or banking—is America's biggest industry. Each year $50 billion is bet illegally on baseball, football, and basketball. Another $7 billion is wagered legally at state-run race tracks and jai alai frontons. Up to fifteen times that figure is bet illegally with bookmakers on horses. Another $5 billion is bet annually on the numbers racket. Countless millions change hands in private games of poker, backgammon, gin rummy, bridge, and craps and such one-on-one betting as elections, golf matches and other propositions. Nevada casino grosses top $1 billion annually; illegal joints across the country match or surpass that figure.

Not only is gambling big, but it is a growth industry. We are in the middle of a gambling boom, partly created by the recession, but primarily caused by the increase in the amount of leisure time most Americans are experiencing.

1

But while gambling is on the upswing, so is losing. The average gambler is a loser. He spends his life being fleeced because he does not know enough about the game he's playing, does not know his chances of winning, and does not know when to bet and when to back off.

In some ways the average gambler is afraid of winning. The work ethic and religious teachings have cast moral doubts on "getting something for nothing." Many gamblers do not feel quite right about winning. Losing is the price they pay for the sin of wagering. The common thought is that you cannot win any game of chance unless you cheat or you are just plain lucky. Most would deny the desire (or courage) to cheat and luck cannot be controlled, so most gamblers resign themselves to a lifetime of losing and casting ethical aspersions on the successful gamblers. The public image of gamblers is certainly warped. The successful gambler is a swarthy, cigar-chomping goon who talks out of the side of his mouth— one step removed from a child molester. The unsuccessful gambler's image is more ordinary—he's a compulsive degenerate who only gets his kicks out of losing.

The average gambler may lose more often than he wins, but he does not get a kick out of losing. The average gambler loses because he does not understand the nature of gambling. The possibility of losing is what makes gambling a risk and what makes it thrilling to most people. But the average, unsuccessful gambler is convinced that the only thing that will save him from losing is luck. Reliance on luck, however, is the one thing that will assure defeat.

Winning is a matter of mathematical probability. The smart gambler never bets unless he has an edge—unless the probable payoff exceeds the risk of the wager. There will always be an element of luck in any bet, but the smart gambler reduces to a bare minimum the effect of luck on his chances of winning. As for morality, gambling is merely competition with money as a means of keeping score. Now that churches have endorsed gambling through bingo games and "Las Vegas nights," it would seem that moral crusades against gambling might end. Moral doubts about successful gamblers should end because what separates the successful gambler from the unsuccessful one is not deceit or even superior luck; it is knowledge of the gambling games and the chances of winning in any given situation.

It must be recognized that gambling has led to the financial ruin of many men and women. This is why the first rule of gambling is: Never bet more than you can afford to lose. But losing is not the necessary order of things. While gambling has wiped out fortunes, it has also created them. (Billionaire H.L. Hunt, for example, won his first productive oil well in a poker game.) Whether you win or get wiped out will depend greatly on your adherence to the following rules.

1. Never bet more than you can afford to lose.
2. Avoid all gambling games based totally on chance.
3. Learn a game thoroughly before you gamble on it.
4. Know your chances of winning in all situations.
5. Never bet unless you have an edge, unless the payoff is greater than your chances of winning.
6. Stick to one game—the game you know best.
7. Never play with strangers.
8. Never bet your entire bankroll on one bet.
9. Back off or quit if you are on a losing streak.
10. Never bet when you are tired, sick, drugged, drunk, or emotionally upset.

Bankruptcy is only the ultimate worry when you bet more than you can afford to lose. It also clouds your judgment, changes your manner of play, and can *cause* you to lose. In poker, if you are in obvious financial troubles, the other players will start bluffing you out of pots with alarming regularity. In horse racing you will begin making big bets on favorites and playing it safe in the most dangerous way possible instead of taking the wiser course of betting smaller amounts on likely longshots. Always set a limit on your losses, then quit when you hit that amount.

There are two basic types of gambling: games of chance and games of skill. Games of chance rely solely on luck and while you can improve your chances of winning by knowing the odds and how to bet, you can never reduce the odds against you enough to give you a significant, reasonable edge. Professional gamblers, for this reason, stick to the gambling games where skill can have some effect on predicting or determining the outcome. People are, of course, going to continue betting games of pure chance anyway, so to keep them from financial ruination, there is a section included on such games in this book—how to play them, best systems for betting, and how to improve your chances of winning.

But the gambler's best hope for victory lies elsewhere—in games in which superior knowledge can give you enough of an edge to assure an overall profit. These games, including sports betting, races of horses and dogs, poker and other card games, are games of skill. They also include an element of chance—otherwise they would not belong in a gambling book. This element of chance is what defeats the average gambler. But the successful gambler gets chance to work for him. By knowing a game thoroughly and knowing the odds of winning in any given situation, a gambler can win—if he bets only in situations in which the payoff outweighs the risk. Incidentally, there is a common misconception about odds bets. Most beginning gamblers assume that a $1 bet on a 6-1 proposition will return $6. It will actually return $7. The

4

payoff on any odds bet is your bet plus the odds. A further explanation of payoffs—using the $2 parimutuel bet as a standard—appears in Appendix A.

The premise of *The Gambler's Bible* is that anyone can gamble and win. Most losing gamblers have blamed their losses on inferior luck. Luck, in the long run, should have nothing to do with it. This is not to deny the existence of luck; everyone has had good and bad streaks of fortune. But there is no way to make that good-luck streak last; and there is no way you can stop a bad streak. Luck cannot be changed or created. Luck cannot be counted on, but the law of averages can. If you play only when the odds are with you, eventually you will win. If you ignore the percentages and play against the odds, no matter how lucky you are, the law of averages will ultimately grind you down.

Most successful or professional gamblers try to specialize in one game or two related games. A good poker player concentrates all his efforts on developing his poker-playing skill. Playing the horses will tend to dissipate his energies. And while he still may play poker well, he is likely to lose much of his poker winnings on the horses because of insufficient knowledge about horse racing. The legendary gambler Titanic Thompson once won close to $1 million by playing poker in San Francisco, then dumped the whole bundle trying to beat the horses in New York. Only bet big on the game you know.

The game you specialize in should be suited to your personality; not all the beatable games will be equally attractive to each gambler. Personality plays an important part in deciding success in certain games. In poker, for example, a player has to suppress his emotions throughout a game or he will tip his cards and strategy to his opponents. Beating roulette calls for infinite patience since the player has to watch the roulette wheel for hours trying to catch biases in the wheel. Many thoroughbred horse players (this writer included) cannot stand harness racing. Hobbled-up horses pulling carts single file seems to pale next to the thoroughbreds. Gambling should be profitable and fun. So study and play the games you enjoy best—so long as they are not games based totally on chance and you can get ready access to them.

After you do know a game well enough to play it, do not blow all that study by playing with strangers or betting stupidly. If you are betting sports—baseball, football, etc.—make sure someone you trust has vouched for your bookie. It can be very frustrating if your bookmaker takes a powder just after you made a big killing on the Super Bowl. Never gamble at cards with strangers—they will cheat you on every possible hand. Likewise avoid private crap games with strangers, particularly if someone seems to be winning an inordinate amount of the time. You have to be quick to spot loaded dice; it is better to avoid this kind of game altogether.

Winning at gambling is always based on percentages. Depending on the odds and the game, if you make a certain number of bets on a certain proposition, you will be guaranteed a certain profit percentage. But you will never be able to guarantee that the next bet will win—just that over hundreds of plays you will win more money than you lose. By betting the entire bankroll on one play, you are counting on luck, and no successful gambler can do that. There are no sure things in gambling.

Gambling requires a cool head. Decisions have to be made according to your chances of winning, not according to your need to break even for the day or the year. Always set a limit on your losses and once you have lost that, quit. Always reassess your playing when you are on a losing streak. You may be playing badly because you are tired or upset, or sick, or whatever. Everyone has days when nothing goes right. Do not gamble unless you have a clear mind—you will only lose.

All of the prominent gambling games are covered thoroughly in this book—how to play, how to beat them, when to bet, and when not to bet. The reader will learn how to make his own point spreads for football and basketball; updated methods for handicapping baseball; why, contrary to most gambling books, thoroughbred horse racing can be beaten; how to beat roulette and private craps; how to win at poker, blackjack, baccarat, rummy and other card games; and which gambling games to avoid. In addition *The Gambler's Bible* is the first general gambling book to show how to beat jai alai, dog racing, quarterhorse racing, backgammon, and harness horse racing. Each of these gambling games has been enjoying phenomenal growth in the past five years; these are the gambling games of the future, and as in the other more common games in which superior knowledge provides a winning edge, these games can also be beaten. *The Gambler's Bible* will also advise you on how to win election bets and how to avoid being a sucker when somebody offers you the bet of a lifetime.

It has been estimated that 90 percent of all people who gamble are lifetime losers. It is time to join the other 10 percent.

1

Horse Racing

Most general gambling books claim that the races cannot be beaten because of the tax bite and track takeout imposed on all winning bets. This takeout ranges from 14 to 25 percent, depending on the track or the type of bet. (So-called exotic bets like the triple, in which the bettor selects the first three horses in exact order, are often taxed at 25 percent.) This takeout is frequently described as a "house advantage" that the gambler is working against and is compared unfavorably to house advantages in such games as roulette, where the takeout is only 5.26 percent. Because of this race track bite, gambling experts like John Scarne claim that "beating the horses is an impossibility in the long run." Scarne is wrong. And in this chapter you will find out why. You will also see the holes in his and other experts' recommendations for betting on the horses.

The problem with comparing the track takeout to the house advantage in casino games is that odds are based on different factors. In roulette, for instance, there are thirty-eight numbers on the American wheel, including the 0 and 00 held by the house, yet the house pays off at 35-1. Unless the wheel is biased, it is a mathematical certainty, based on the law of averages, that the house will win two out of every thirty-eight times (based on thousands of revolutions of the wheel) or 5.26 percent of the time. To repeat, the payoff is only 35-1, but the odds of hitting any one number are one in thirty-eight. That is the house advantage.

In parimutuel betting, the computerized system used by the tracks, the money bet on each animal minus the state and track cut, determines the odds. Thus, the odds are set by public whim and may or may not reflect the horse's actual chances of winning. In a given race, for example, a horse may be a natural 2-1 shot, which means because of his ability compared to that of the other horses in the race, the likelihood of his winning is one out of three (a 2-1 payoff is $6). But his actual odds may be 6-1 or 6-5. If you bet the horse at 6-5, you are a sucker. If you bet it at 6-1, you can beat the races, gambling authorities to the contrary. The horse still has the same chances of winning, but your probable payoff has more than doubled. (6-1 pays $14 to win.) If you bet only overlays (horses at odds higher than their chances of winning), you can beat the track takeout.

Yet Scarne and other so-called experts recommend playing favorites. Scarne suggests betting favorites to show so that the bettor will not get hurt too much at the track. (The standard bets in all forms of horse racing are win, place, and show. A win ticket pays if the horse finishes first; a place ticket pays if the horse finishes first or second; and a show ticket pays if the horse comes in first, second, or third, which is called finishing "in the money." Because of the reduced risks on place and show tickets, the payoffs are usually much lower than win payoffs. The minimum bet at the track is $2; payoffs published are to $2, though bets are available in denominations above that.)

Year after year, track after track, 60 to 65 percent of all favorites finish in the money, thus paying a show price.

In order to break even, however, the show prices have to average $3; that rarely happens with favorites. In fact it is a near certainty that you will lose steadily by betting favorites to show. Another popular book recommends placing only win bets on the favorite, claiming that while the bettor will not win, he will cash a few tickets and wind up only a few dollars down. Only one third of all favorites win; to break even, the win prices have to average $6 to compensate for the two-thirds losers. This will never happen. With this system you will lose more money faster, but any system of betting favorites is a sure way to lose, whether you bet them to win, place, or show.

No one who consistently plays only favorites can make a profit at the race track. And to this writer there is little sense in betting if you are planning to lose. Expecting to lose is what makes bookies rich and 90 percent of all gamblers lifetime losers. All it takes to beat the races is knowledge of handicapping each type of race and the bettor's refusal to bet any animal whose odds drop below that of his chances of winning. (Handicapping is the science of predicting the outcome of a race based on the past performances of the participants in that race.)

There are two major forms of horse racing: thoroughbreds and standardbreds, or harness racing. Most gambling books ignore harness racing and concentrate on what they consider the risks of betting on thoroughbreds. This book will correct that oversight on standardbreds and counter the malignment of thoroughbreds, because both sports can be beaten and they offer the easiest access to legal gambling opportunities for the average man or woman. This chapter will cover in detail handicapping methods for thoroughbred and harness horse racing, plus advice on how and when to bet, how to tell what odds a horse is worth, how to tell if a race has been fixed, and what types of races to avoid.

THOROUGHBRED HORSE RACING

Damon Runyon to the contrary, not all horse players die broke. H.L. Hunt used to net $1 million a year off his horse playing. Art Rooney, owner of the Pittsburgh Steelers football team, was just another struggling sports promoter until he won over $150,000 on a single afternoon at Saratoga race track in the 1930s, thus providing the initial boost to his personal fortune. Isadore Bieber used his winnings at the race track to finance the most successful racing stable of mid-century America, a stable that included such stars as the near-millionaire Styme and the leading stallion Hail to Reason. Pittsburgh Phil left an estate worth millions at his death. The list could run on and on, but these few examples should suffice. Horse playing can be profitable.

These horse players made their biggest killings in the days before parimutuel betting. There were certain advantages to betting with bookmakers. The bookies' cut was less than the current track takeout; you could shop for odds among the various bookies; and once you placed your bet, the odds would not change on your wager, even if the bookie later changed the odds for that horse on succeeding bets. Today you can go quietly crazy as that 4-1 shot you bet five minutes ago is bet down to 6-5.

But the races still can be beaten. Every race track has its coterie of professional gamblers. Several more race track millionaires have been created. This book cannot promise to make you one of them, but strict attention to the rules and methods described can cut your losses and should provide a steady profit at the races.

There are three basic keys to winning under parimutuels:

1. The public does not know what it is doing.
2. Pace makes the race.
3. Do not bet a horse at odds less than what he is worth.

Odds under parimutuel betting are determined by the amount of money bet on each horse minus the state and track takeout. To further explain this, consider a two-horse race at a track where the total takeout (state tax, city tax, track cut, and horsemen's cut) is 17 percent. The handle—or total amount bet on both horses—for the race is $100,000. The track takes its 17 percent cut or $17,000 off the top and then repays $83,000 to those patrons who hold winning tickets. If $50,000 is bet on each horse, their actual odds are even. Without the tax cut, the winners would receive $2 for each $1 bet; the losers would, of course, get nothing. But, under parimutuels, there is only $83,000 to split among the winning bettors. If there were twenty-five thousand $2 winning tickets, this means each bettor would receive a payoff of $3.32. The track, however, also collects breakage, which means it rounds off the number to the nearest and lowest 20-cent divisible figure. So the payoff is only $3.20. This cut then is really 80 cents out of $4 or 20 percent with breakage on this bet. This is certainly a disadvantage to the bettor, but there is one saving grace. While the track's huge cut will reduce the odds on each horse, the fact that the public creates those odds in the first place can work for you. The public will very commonly bet down to favoritism a horse that cannot win and will virtually ignore a horse that cannot lose. The public choice, or favorite, loses two-thirds of the time. It is in those two-thirds of the races that you will make your profit.

The favorite is often a false favorite because the public, in general, does not understand pace. Pace is the manner in which a race is run: which horses run on the lead, which horses lie within striking distance behind the leaders, which horses come from behind, fast starters and slow starters, sprinters and distance horses. Most horses develop running habits when they are young and these rarely vary. Certain trainers will train all their horses to start fast and grab the lead; others will train their horses to stay behind and gain ground in the stretch. Other horses will invariably prompt the pace, ready within striking distance to take over from tiring front-runners. Each race can be looked upon as a puzzle. Your job is to gauge and compare the running styles of the participants in the race and fit each in the race according to such factors as condition, class, track condition, distance, weight, track biases, jockeys, etc. The pace of the race will be determined by these factors as well as by running style.

Finally, you should never bet a horse at odds less than what he is worth. Consider that two horse race again. If both horses are equal, then the odds should be even. But because of the track takeout, each horse is at 3-5. The bet is not worth it. Never bet a horse if your expected payoff is less than the chances of his winning. Supposing the horses are still equal but one horse is at even odds, the bet then becomes equal to his chances of winning. But again he is not worth it. In order to make a profit, the gambler has to have an edge on each bet. A merely fair bet is not enough. If the odds are 6-5, the bet is worth it. The payoff is now $4.40 for a 10 percent profit. Or if one of the 3-5 shots is twice as good as the other, the better horse is a sensible wager. When the odds provide you a profit over what the horse's ideal payoff should be, that is called an overlay. Never bet any horse that is not an overlay.

How do you determine pace and catch overlays? It is necessary to start with the basic factors used for handicapping horse races. First, become closely acquainted with the *Daily Racing Form*. The *Form* is the only reliable source of information on the past performances of all horses running at all thoroughbred tracks in North America. The price is $1—a bit steep for a newspaper— but it is absolutely essential. Most of the information you need will be included in the section called Past Performances. This section records the most recent finishes of each horse in every race scheduled for that day at the thoroughbred track in the city in which it is sold. (It also includes past performances for other regional tracks.) The record includes the last eight to ten races, where the horse was in relation to the leaders at several points during each race, the final position, the final and fractional times for each race, the distances, jockeys, weight carried, class of each race, latest workouts, conditions of current race, etc. In short, everything you need to know about how a horse runs, in which class he runs best, and what condition he is in on that particular day. This record will help you determine each horse's chances in a race according to the major factors.

The factors involved in determining the outcome of a race include: class, consistency, condition, running habits, jockey, weight, trainer, distance, appearance, equipment changes, relative speed, track surface, track condition, post position, finish in last race, and recent workouts. A description of each factor and how it figures in the outcome of a race follows.

Class

There are four basic types of thoroughbred horse races: stakes or handicaps; allowances; claiming; and maiden races. The stakes races are the classiest; they attract the best horses because they offer the highest purses. Stakes races include such well-known events as the Kentucky Derby or the Belmont Stakes. Entry in these events requires payment of an entry fee by a horse's owner; the entry fees are added to the purse and split among the first four finishers.

An allowance race is just below a stakes race in class. (Though it must be stressed that a New York allowance horse will be classier than, say a Midwest stakes horse, because the New York horse has been running for higher purses, against stiffer competition.) Allowance races are condition races. A typical allowance condition may limit the race to nonwinners of three races, with a weight allowance for weaker horses in the race. This is done to create a fairly equal race.

Claiming races provide the bulk of racing in the United States. A claiming race is assigned a price—say $25,000—and all horses entered in that race are eligible to be "claimed" or bought, at that price. Claims must be posted before the race and at most tracks horses can only be claimed by owners or trainers who have started at least one horse at the current meeting of that particular track. In California, there is an open claiming rule—anybody can buy the horse at the price offered. The claiming race is essential for providing races for the cheaper, more populous stock at each track.

Assigning a price to a race also is aimed at evening out a race. In a $10,000 claiming race, for example, most of the horses will be worth somewhere around $10,000. If the horse is worth more, he may be very likely to dominate the field, but someone will buy him at the reduced price. If he is worth less, he will have a slim chance of winning. So trainers try to spot their horses low enough for the horse to have a chance, but high enough to get a fair price if someone does put in a claim.

A maiden race is a race between non-winners. When a horse wins his first race, this is referred to in race track parlance as "breaking his maiden." One win makes a horse ineligible for maiden races. There are two types of maiden races: maiden claimers and maiden special weights. In maiden claimers a price is assigned to a race, and all horses are eligible to be purchased at that price. Maiden special weight races are the maiden equivalent of allowance races. All horses are weighted the same, however. These are the more well-regarded younger horses on the tracks, the horses who are expected to fill the allowance and stakes ranks.

Generally speaking, a stakes horse will beat an allowance horse, an allowance horse will beat a claimer, and everyone will beat a maiden claimer. But there are exceptions. Some allowance races are run for lower purses than higher-priced claimers. For example, a typical New York weekday allowance race might offer a purse of $10,000 and be eligible to nonwinners of two races. A $30,000 to $35,000 (claiming races often have a top and bottom price; horses get weight off for entering at the lower price) claiming race may be set for older horses the same day, with the purse at $15,000. The competition is a lot stiffer in the latter race since each of these horses has several wins and loads of experience. The allowance horses, however, have not proved themselves; each has only managed to win a maiden race.

It is a good practice to keep records of purses offered and the conditions of each race at your track. This is essential not only to gauge the differences between cheap allowance or high-level claimers, but also to determine class within the divisions themselves. At the smaller tracks, for example, it is quite common for most of the races to be run at a single, rock-bottom claiming price—usually $1500. But not all those claimers are equal and the casual bettor has a tendency to pay attention only to the price and not the conditions of the race. One race may be a $1500 claimer for nonwinners of four races in 1975, another might be a $1500 claimer for nonwinners of two races, lifetime.

Consider a race in which the two major contenders have come from the above races. The horse from the latter race won it decisively. The horse from the former race faded in the stretch. The Past Performances only contain the $1500 price and not the level of competition or the possible difference in purse. In the above example, the recent winner would go off as the favorite, but the classier horse is the more likely winner. The same situation prevails among allowance races—the conditions and the purse of the race determine its class, but the Past Performances can only fit in the word "allowance." Keeping records is essential and it will put you ahead of 95 percent of your fellow horse players.

An exception to the class rule is the improving horse. Younger horses—two-year olds and three-year olds—are particularly able to go up in class. Their trainers may have underestimated their ability or the horse just suddenly gets the hang of racing. Catching the improving horse is one of the hardest parts of handicapping—it is also the most lucrative. The public disregards horses going up in class; the lowest odds are on horses going down in class, yet they are no more likely to win. (Each type wins about 20 percent of all races; the bulk of winners come from horses staying in the same class.)

How do you catch an improving horse? Watch a horse that raced gamely in his last race despite excuses. Watch a horse that has been racing greenly or poorly, but made up a significant amount of ground in the stretch of its last race. Watch a horse that has been foundering on muddy or sloppy tracks once it gets to a fast track. In a turf race, watch a horse if his first race on that surface seemed to bring him to life. Watch a horse that gets a significant jockey change. Watch a horse that has had consistently poor starts, yet burst first or second out of the gate in its last race. Watch a horse that has decisively won its last race, overpowering the cheaper field. These horses are all eligible to move up in class. Also, respect a horse with high early speed if there are no other front-running horses in the race, even if the horse seems to be out-classed.

As for horses moving down in class, do not over-estimate them. The public is too fond of class dropdowns. Yet, in claiming races particularly, a dropdown may not be aimed at winning a part of the purse, but at unloading a tired, possibly lame, horse on some other unsuspecting trainer. Beware of a horse dropping down drastically if it lost gound in the stretch in its last race but has not worked since, or has had one dismal workout. Remember that a horse going from an allowance to a claimer is not always dropping down. Check the purses and conditions of each race. Also remember that a horse's class is not determined by the type of horses he has been racing against, but the class of horses he can beat or run in the money against. A horse who has been running and losing badly in $20,000 claiming races is not a $20,000 horse, and if his next race is a $15,000 claimer, this is not a reduction in class. Find out in his record where he wins—that's his class.

Finally, maidens—even promising maidens—rarely win against winners. Unless you have inside information, do not bet maidens against winners, particularly in al-lowance or stakes races.

Consistency

Some horses hate to win; they feel lonely out there ahead of the pack, so they will pull up and wait for the other horses, relinquishing the lead. Some horses are crazy, some are indifferent, and others will run their hearts out no matter what class they are running in. These

19

latter horses will win their share of races when placed in the right class. You will be ahead of the game, however, if you avoid the inconsistent horse. An inconsistent horse is one that never seems to win, even though it places in the money frequently. An inconsistent horse wins less than 10 percent of the time or places in the money less than 25 percent of its races. Cheaper horses, particularly, rarely win back to back; their records show few good races and a lot of poor ones. They cannot be trusted to always try. Avoid horses who do not seem to win. If the significantly best horse in the race is inconsistent and in condition, it is best to pass the race. Do not get into guessing games. Give a special edge to any horse that wins 25 percent or more of his races, comes in the money 50 percent or more of the time, and seems to race well each time he is entered in the proper class.

Condition

Only horses in condition win horse races. The best horse in the race may be running poorly; he may be fat or tired. He will probably lose because winners have to be sharp. It is fairly simple to determine if a horse is in shape. First, glance at his recent record. Did he finish in the money or within five lengths of the leaders in his last race? Did he make up five lengths or more in the stretch of his last race? Was he in front or within three lengths of the leaders at the half-mile pole of his last race? (This is the second call listed in the Past Performances in the *Daily Racing Form* for sprint races and the first call for distance races.) If he did not run well in the last race, did he have an excuse? (This would include muddy or sloppy tracks; being outclassed, blocked, impeded; stumbled start, etc.) Has he worked out since his last race? (Workout lines are the bottom entry of each horse's Past Performance chart in the *Form*.) If the horse has shown any sign of life in its last race, it is probably in racing condition.

It may not be in winning condition, however. If the horse has been fading in the stretch lately and is showing poor workouts or no workouts at all, consider it past its peak condition. The horse is tailing off and should be rested a bit. Most horses are raced into shape in North America (the exception is high-class horses which are trained to be ready for each start). Trainers are out to make a quick buck; tracks have to fill races. So horses use races to get into condition. Do not expect a horse to be in peak condition after racing poorly for a long time and then showing one flash of life. Watch out for a horse that gradually improves. Horses that "wake up" in one race cannot be trusted.

Finish in Last Race

Finish in the last race is related to condition. Most races are won by horses that finished first or second in their last start. In a race among cheap stock, horses that finished second are more likely to prevail over horses that finished first in their last race because cheap horses race into peak condition, but do not maintain that shape for long. If a horse finished in the money or within five lengths of the winner and had an excuse in his last race, expect him to do well in his next one. If a horse shows gameness in the face of adversity, this gameness should carry over to the next race.

Workouts

Workouts are another indication of condition. Horses are exercised every day, but are only asked for speed about once a week. This speed trial is called a workout. A standard workout will run about twelve seconds per furlong (a furlong is one-eighth mile). Cheaper tracks will average slower workouts. A horse should work out at least once a week. If a horse returns to race seven days or more after its last contest, it should show at least one workout. If it does not, be suspicious. If the workout is much slower than the horse usually works out, also be suspicious. Workouts will vary from horse to horse— some horses run well in the afternoon but will not move in the morning. If a horse has a very slow workout, do not discount it. If it is a cheap horse, give it credit that it was worked out at all. Otherwise compare the workout to others listed for it in the Past Performances. Only worry about a discrepancy. Some trainers work their charges away from the track and public clockers, so no workouts will be published. Again, do not discount a horse that has not worked out, if the records show no public workouts at any time in its recent career.

Date of Last Race

Cheap horses will go stale after a layoff of more than two weeks; allowance horses and high-level claimers should race again within three weeks in order to assure top condition in their current race. Horses off two months or more rarely win (except stakes horses, which are trained into condition) because horses are raced into shape. Most winners have run within two weeks prior to the winning race. If a cheap horse's last race was impressive, but the trainer waited more than two weeks to race the animal again, be suspicious. That last good race probably took too much out of him. To be a contender this horse should have several sharp workouts since that last race. Be suspicious of a high-level claimer or allowance horse that waits more than three weeks to race again. The same logic applies to this type of horse. Bringing a horse back to the races within five days of its last start is a good sign that a horse is fit and the trainer thinks he is ready to win. Make sure, however, that the horse is relatively fresh and has not started more than six times in the last two months.

Physical Appearance

The final indicator of condition is physical appearance. If a horse is wearing high bandages on his front legs, watch out. This is a sign of tendon trouble and the horse could break down or pull up lame. High bandages on the back legs could be an indication of muscle problems, but are not particularly worrisome since the front legs get all the action. Short bandages on front or back legs are called "rundowns" and just prevent the horse from scraping its ankles on the track.

If a horse looks dull, pass it by. Dull means a coat that is not shiny, eyes that are lifeless, or a drooping head. If the horse keeps trying to throw its rider, is excessively skittish or fractious or all lathered up, pass it by. This horse is leaving its race in the paddock. He will only win if he is ten lengths better than the field. Also pass by a horse in the following circumstances: A horse that keeps throwing its head up and down while walking may be in pain. A horse that keeps making strange movements with its mouth, baring its teeth, may be fighting the bit. If the horse is limping or even walking stiffly, he will run badly. Any of these situations can cost a race. This is why it is essential to see the horses before they run. A horse may look like a sure thing on paper, but on the day of the race, he just may not feel like running. It costs you nothing to pass up the race.

Running Habits

As mentioned earlier most horses settle into running patterns that they rarely abandon. A front running horse will always try for the lead; a faster horse may beat him to it or his own jockey may try to cure him of the habit, but the horse will try. That is where he feels most comfortable racing. Likewise the come-from-behind horse feels most comfortable laying back until the end of the race. The jockey might try to move him faster, but the horse will probably fight him.

The front-running horse will win if he is unchallenged for the lead, or is much classier than the horse or horses that challenge him for the lead. The front-runner also stands a better chance of winning, even if challenged, if he is running on a track that favors speed horses such as the cement-like tracks of the West and Southwest. In the East, the sand is deeper and a horse is more likely to fade.

The come-from-behind horse will win only if there is enough speed up front to set up the race for him by tiring out the other contenders, or if the race is too long for the other contenders. If a speed horse is allowed to set his own pace, the late-running horse will not be able to make it up in time. The come-from-behind horse will often lose even if he is the best horse in the race because he lagged too far behind and another horse was allowed to "steal" the race by grabbing and holding the lead.

The third type of horse is the pace prompter. He starts well, lies back third or fourth, and is ready to take over from the tiring leader or leaders. This horse needs no specific conditions to win the race, unlike the front runner and off-the-pace horse. He will be defeated if one horse is allowed to take an unchallenged lead, or, if there is an honest pace, if the come-from-behind horse is simply classier. (This is assuming that the horse is in condition.)

Most horse races are won by animals that stalk the pace.

Front-runners win more often in sprints; come-from-behind horses have a better chance in distance races. Another aspect of running style is the start. Horses each have gate habits. Some consistently start well; others lose the race at the start. In sprints, particularly, a quick start is essential. Even with a come-from-behind horse, a smart jockey gets him out of the gate fast in order to put him in good position, so he will have running room when the big move starts. Avoid bad starters in sprints unless the horse is getting a new jockey—one with a reputation for getting his horses out fast.

Distance

Thoroughbred horse races are held at distances from three furlongs to two miles and beyond. A sprint race is anything under a mile; a distance race is anything over that. A mile race is considered a sprint if it is only around one turn; a distance race if around two turns. Some horses are equally good at several distances, but most are limited to one distance. A six-furlong horse will often fade at seven furlongs and tire badly at a mile. A distance horse will not get into gear until the last quarter of a sprint. Before betting a horse, determine the animal's suitability to the distance. Has he raced and won at this distance before? Is this a better distance for him? A horse with early speed may have been running a series of distance races, tiring in each. If he is now entered in a sprint, the logical assumption is that he should win at this distance. Unfortunately, however, those distance races may have dulled his speed. The early fractions of route races are at least a full second slower than the early fractions of a sprint. The horse may find it hard to catch up to the sprinters the first time back. This is something to be aware of

25

when a front-running distance horse is put into a sprint. If he runs his usual fractions, he will be at least five lengths behind at the quarter. Do not count on this type of horse to kill off another front-runner.

A second thing to look out for is the come-from-behind sprinter. It would seem from the way he finishes that he wants a longer distance. This is not necessarily so. The off-the-pace habit is only his running style and has nothing to do with his stamina. The horse may just not have what it takes to go a longer distance. Do not bet on it. He may win, but you are only guessing. Do not bet unless he has shown some previous ability to win at the distance.

Jockeys

You do not have to be smart to be a jockey; you have to be short. The best jockeys are small and intelligent, but the average jockey is just taking advantage of nature's oversight in the size department. It has been said that the outcome of a horse race is 90 percent horse and 10 percent jockey. That 10 percent looms large if there are two contenders—one with a superior rider, the other with an untalented one. Riding is not easy; it takes experience, courage, poise, and the ability to think fast. A slow-witted jockey will get your horse boxed in every chance he gets. An inexperienced jockey cannot control the horse when the animal starts tiring, as almost all horses do toward the end of a race. Do not bet apprentice jockeys unless they are in the top jockey standings, have otherwise proven themselves adequate to the task, or the horse is much the best. (An apprentice is a young jockey, just learning the trade; to allow for inexperience, each horse an apprentice rides is given a weight break. The size of the break depends on how many races the apprentice has won. The break is ten pounds before the fifth victory, seven pounds until the thirty-fifth, then five pounds thereafter until one year has passed after the fifth win, when the apprenticeship ends. The apprentice is given no break in stakes races.)

Certain jockeys are better at breaking their horses fast out of the gate. Keep records of this on the jockeys at your track and when betting on sprints, avoid jockeys who constantly start badly.

A final word of warning about jockeys. They are no more honest than anyone else. If a jockey stands to make more money by throwing a race than he can by winning, do not be surprised if he succumbs to temptation. Particularly on triple or exacta (exotic betting) races, be very wary of the favorite. The horse's jockey may not throw it, but the other riders can block him to keep the favorite out of the money.

In a triple, the bet is to pick the exact one-two-three finish. If the favorites are kept out of the money, the winning tickets are worth thousands. In exactas, the bet is to pick the exact one-two finish. These tickets can reach payoffs of several hundred dollars if the favorite is stiffed. The jockeys, even at major tracks, do fix these races. Do not believe the malarkey that they have too much to lose by being dishonest. A jockey's professional life is limited; it is a dangerous profession and any additional tax-free cash he can stock away makes the post-forty destitution, that has hit so many of them, that much less likely. Many jockeys will not join in fixing races, but they will not blow the whistle on those who do. All these exotic bets in which a $2 bet can win thousands have increased cheating. The only safeguard you have is to avoid betting in triple or exacta races unless your horse is an outsider.

Trainers

The trainer is hired by the owner to condition and race the horse. Trainers, like jockeys, have varying degrees of talent. It is best to favor a horse whose trainer has a good win percentage. Beware of horse-killer trainers—those who race their horses week in and week out, never allowing a rest, winding up with twenty-five to thrity races per horse by early fall. These trainers will rarely win even if they drop their charges into a lower class—horses do not win once they are tired and stale.

Some trainers are very involved in the betting end of the business—particularly at the smaller tracks where it is tough to make a living on the purses alone. The trainer who wants to cash a bet on his horse will pull a trick called darkening a horse's form. The trainer gets his horse in shape and ready to win. It is fairly obvious from his recent races that the horse is ready, but the trainer knows the horse will hold its peak for awhile. So he enters the horse in a race (or two) that is totally unsuitable. The horse bombs out and all the public sees is that dismal finish. After one or more unsuitable races, the trainer decides that the horse's condition will be sufficiently suspect in the mind of the public. Then he enters the horse where he belongs. The horse goes off at 12-1 and the trainer makes a bundle when the horse wins. So it is imperative for the handicapper to determine where the horse belongs in relation to distance, class, etc. before discounting him on apparent poor recent form.

Weight

Weight is often overemphasized as a factor in defeating a horse. Pay attention to weight only in these circumstances: the track is sloppy, muddy, or good; a soft, yielding, good track if it is the turf course; a horse that has never carried this weight successfully in the past; or a substantial seven or more pounds weight difference between two contenders (unless the weight break is caused by apprentice allowance).

Equipment Changes

Equipment changes include getting blinkers on or off, dispensing with the whip, or putting on horseshoes with mud calks. Blinker changes can result in significant improvement with a younger horse or a horse that tends to run on the lead and fade. The change can cause a horse to relax better or pay greater attention to the business of racing. A trainer will sometimes ban his jockey from using a whip in order to turn around a sulky horse. Avoid this horse, and avoid the race if he is a contender. This is introducing an unknown factor.

Mud calks are used on off tracks and turf races so that the horse can grip the surface better (calks are the horse equivalent of cleats on baseball shoes). It can be an important factor if one contender has calks and the other does not. But it will not make a winner out of a pig.

Post Position

Post position does not usually play much importance in thoroughbred racing except in one circumstance. If the start of a race is near the turn, favor inside horses, particularly one with early speed. The outside horses will lose a great deal of ground on the run to the first turn. Their jockeys may have to use them earlier than desired in order to keep up with or ahead of the pack. If there are two early speed horses in a race, in general favor the horse on the inside because it will lose less ground on the turn.

29

Relative Speed

Speed means little in thoroughbred racing except at tracks with hard surfaces. Cheap horses set track records every day, but they run out of the money when they face better, supposedly slower horses. Final times do not mean a thing. However, fractional times may help you determine the pace of the race. If one early-speed horse consistently runs the first quarter in 23 seconds and another runs it in 22 2/5, the latter horse will have a three length lead at the quarter. But which horse wins the race to the quarter is more a reflection of class. The better horse will likely be running consistently faster races.

Tracks with hard surfaces favor early speed, and the horse with the fastest average final time may often win a sprint. But again, this is primarily a reflection of class and the effect it and track biases have on pace.

Track Biases

Some tracks favor speed; other tracks have holding surfaces that favor come-from-behind horses. Certain post positions will never win; others will win more than their share. There is only one way to discern the current bias of the track you attend. No book or magazine can do it for you because tracks have a tendency to change from year to year and season to season. Keep these records for the first ten days of the meeting: winning post positions at each distance, percentage of fast starters winning, and winning running styles at each distance. This should give you the track biases.

Track Surface

There are two basic track surfaces: dirt and turf. Turf races are run on grass tracks, contained within the dirt pearance, current condition, jockey, running style, con-

tracks at the major North American race courses. In Europe there are only turf races. Turf races in America are often easier to handicap because: 1) the horses are sounder and more consistent; 2) once they have reached a certain class, they stay there; and 3) the races are usually distance races, minimizing the effect of bad racing luck or poor starts on the outcome.

Track Condition

The most common track condition is fast; an off-track can be slow, good, muddy, or sloppy. A turf course can be firm, good, soft, yielding, or hard. All horses have track condition idiosyncracies. Never bet a race unless each horse in condition shows at least one race on the track condition for today's race.

Age and Sex

Horses do not become fully developed until midway in their third year; some horses take even longer. So until at least August, a three-year-old horse will be at a disadvantage against older, more mature animals. Do not bet a three-year-old against older horses unless he has shown previous ability to whip his elders.

Fillies do not beat colts unless they are greatly superior. Do not bet a filly or a mare (older female horse) against male horses unless she has shown a previous ability to beat male horses.

Betting

The probable winner of any particular race is the horse that best fits the conditions of the race (distance, class, track condition, surface, post position) without being eliminated by any of the other factors (physical apsistency). In many races there will be no solid selection because there are too many unknown factors or because competition will throw the race up for grabs. Do not bet a race unless one horse has a solid edge. Or, if there are only two contenders and the odds are high enough to make a profit, bet them both to win.

Even if you do zero in on a solid choice, in parimutuel betting it is not enough just to bet the probable winner. You have to counter the track takeout and you have to get a reasonable price for your horse. A gambler needs an edge to make a profit, so you must only bet those selections that are underrated by the public. So many things can go wrong in a horse race. The best horse often will not win. You have to allow for these losses and the track takeout by betting only horses that have odds higher than their actual chances of winning. This will drastically limit the number of your bets, but it will just as drastically increase your profits. The best horse in the race will win about 35 to 40 percent of the time, whether it is at 3-5 or 3-1, but it only pays to bet the overlay.

But when does a horse become an overlay? Legendary horse player Jule Fink, the man who developed pace handicapping, never bet a horse below 3-1 odds. The reasoning here is that if your handicapping turns one horse as the best in the race, it will have to be worth at least 3-1. This is not a bad way of catching overlays, but it may limit your betting even further. I would adjust that figure for small fields and for horses with an obvious early speed advantage. In small fields, six horses or less, the odds will necessarily be reduced because of the lack of betting interests. Fit the odds to the size of the field in this manner: in a six-horse field, do not bet below 5-2; for a five-horse field, 2-1; and in a four-horse field, 8-5. If your horse is the only early speed horse in the race, his chances of winning are significantly increased. Allow slightly lower odds, but increase your bets on odds of 3-1 or more.

Always bet win and place; bet show on odds of 8-1 or above. The reason for lowering your bets on favorites is that favorites are more likely to be stiffed. A higher odds horse is a better risk for this reason. A higher odds horse will also net you a profit if he comes in second; the place winnings will generally pay off more than $4. It is wise to up your potential profits. On those high odds horses, you may even make a profit or at least break even if the horse hangs on for third. The idea is not necessarily to pick the winner, but to make a profit on your bets.

There is also a wide array of exotic bets available in horse racing, ranging from the staid daily double to triples and double exactas. These bets are at $2 and $5 and promise high profits for small investments. The daily double means selecting the winners of the first two races; an exacta selects the first two horses in a race in the exact order; a double exacta selects exactas in two successive races; a triple selects the first three finishers in exact order. These special bets rarely pay off at the actual chances of hitting and are not recommended unless you have solid selections. Only bet a daily double if you have a logical good selection for both races. Do not "wheel" a sure thing in the first with every horse in the second race. "Wheeling" the daily double means buying a ticket on your horse in the first or second race combined with every horse in the half of the daily double. If you feel horse #2 is a sure thing in the first, for example, to "wheel" him you will buy daily double tickets on the 2-1, 2-2, 2-3, 2-4, 2-5, 3-6, 2-7, etc. combinations. If your horse wins the first, you win the daily double since you have combined him with all the horses in the second. If your horse loses, your entire investment is shot. The risks outweigh the possible payoff. Sure things often lose.

In exacta betting, only bet if you have narrowed the race to two contenders. Then bet the combination both ways, so that if either horse comes in first and the other runs second, you will win. Do not bet triples. Triple payoffs are much higher than exactas, but luck is the only determining factor. And gamblers should not rely on luck. Another reason to avoid triples is that these races are often fixed. Watch out if your key horse is the favorite. A win is unlikely. If you do make the bet, box the three horses you feel are contenders to get all possible combinations if all three horses do finish in the money. It is impossible to pick the exact order of their finish.

Another way to catch overlays is to weed out the contenders and watch the odds board at the track. Bet a horse if his odds are significantly higher than the morning line. This means the professional handicapper who drew up the morning odds fancied the horse, but the public has backed off. The odds should be lower, so he is an overlay. Only bet him, however, if your own handicapping has shown him to be a contender.

There is only one instance in which you should consider betting a horse that is not an overlay. Take a triple or other exotic race in which there are several possible contenders but in the first flashes of the toteboard, the public has zeroed in on one or two. Write down the odds of each horse after about three minutes of betting has occurred. Then watch the odds board. If one horse gradually goes down in odds—almost with every flash— this generally means the professional money is going down on that horse. The fix is in. He may not win. Only bet him if you think he is a contender. But these horses win far more often that the stewards, or others who claim racing is completely honest, would care to admit.

On these latter two suggestions, only let the odds board affect your selection if you do not have a strong feeling about which horse should win the race. If you have a solid choice, do not let the public sway you from betting it.

Following is a summary of rules for handicapping horse racing. Some of the admonitions on not betting horses until they are experienced may need explaining. Basically, handicapping is predicting the future from the past. Until a horse's ability, class, and running style have been established, you will only be guessing about what it can do. Guessing relies too much on luck and to be a successful horse player, you have to limit the luck factor as much as possible. Because of luck, you will likely lose more races than you will win. This is why you will only bet overlays—to counter these losses. Betting your opinions will only increase your losses.

1. Never bet your entire bankroll on one race.
2. Do not bet every race.
3. Do not bet a race unless every starter has had at least five races.
4. Do not bet until you can confidently predict the probable pace of a race (which horses will go out front, which horses will come from behind, etc.).
5. Do not accept odds less than a horse's chances of winning.
6. Bet win and place; bet show also if the horse is 8-1 or better.
7. Do not bet with bookies or off-track betting offices; do not bet unless you can see the horses before the race.
8. Avoid races where two or more of the horses are coming off long layoffs and show good workouts, superior class, or previous ability to win after layoffs.
9. Avoid a horse that lost ground in the stretch in his last race, if it does not show workout since.

10. Avoid horses with front-leg bandages.
11. Do not bet turf races in which one or more horses, in condition, have not yet raced on the grass.
12. On off tracks (mud, slop, etc.) avoid any race in which one or more of the horses in condition has not run on muddy or sloppy tracks.
13. Do not bet maidens against winners.
14. Do not bet maiden races when one or more horses are first-time starters.
15. Avoid exotic bets unless the chances of winning justify the probable payoff.
16. Avoid races in which there are too many unknown factors. Eliminate guesswork.
17. Never bet more than you can afford to lose.

HARNESS RACING

Harness racing can be easier to beat than the thoroughbreds. There are fewer factors that determine the outcome of a harness race, and the nature of the sport's fans make it a prime opportunity for catching overlays. Working people have greater access to the night-running trotters than to the daytime thoroughbreds so the competition among bettors is not so stiff. The average harness race fan is a casual bettor out for an evening's fun and willing to pay for it in losing tickets. Thus, anyone with just a small amount of knowledge about harness handicapping is in a great position. (In the land of the blind, the one-eyed man is king.)

In parimutuel betting the gambler has to bet only overlays in order to beat the track takeout and provide himself with an edge. An unsophisticated public will create a high percentage of overlays, and in harness racing the public is far less sophisticated about betting than the average thoroughbred horse player.

The reasons for this are two-fold. First, harness racing is relatively new as a big time sport. And second, literature on how to bet the trotters has not kept pace with the sport's phenomenal recent growth. There is, for instance, no equivalent of the *Daily Racing Form* for trotters. And the magazines devoted to the sport seem divorced from the gambling realities, stressing personalities and pageantry over handicapping.

Most of the major harness tracks have been built in the last thirty-five years. Harness racing was simply a country pastime until lawyer George Morton Levy built Roosevelt Raceway just outside New York City in 1940. Levy poured millions into building harness racing as a major gambling sport. With the development of the mobile starting gate in 1946, harness racing turned one important corner. Prior to that starts were manipulated, constantly called back, or otherwise made to look less than fair or honest to the betting public. But harness racing owes its growth primarily to two factors: the trotters run at night, avoiding competition with the more popular and more established thoroughbreds; and the tracks offer endless opportunities for exotic bets, such as triples, exactas, double exactas and the like, in which the casual bettor could hope to win hundreds or even thousands from a single $2 bet. The promise of nighttime riches, coupled with the leisure-induced gambling boom of the 1960s and 1970s, have pushed harness racing attendance figures toward the 30 million a year mark.

Harness racing would not exist as a major sport were it not for the availability of gambling to its patrons. Some top races are still conducted at small backwater tracks where no betting is permitted. But the attraction of the sport to most fans lies in the gambling opportunities. Certainly the pageantry and much of the grace of thoroughbred racing is missing in harness racing. The horses are not permitted to run; the gaits allowed appear unnatural. The drivers all seem willing to spend most of the race trotting or pacing single file, waiting for a desperate move seventy yards from the finish line. This writer has never failed to be bored at the trotters (but she has also never had a losing night). A gambler who enjoys harness racing would have an even better chance of winning; enthusiasm and personal preference play a great part in learning all the intricacies of a sport. But even for the casual fan, it is extremely easy to learn enough about the trotters to win consistently.

There are two basic types of harness horse: trotters and pacers. The sport is often referred to as "the trotters," but in reality only 25 percent of all harness horses are trotters; the rest are called pacers and have a different racing gait. A harness horse is so-called because it is harnessed to a two-wheeled cart containing a driver. Harness horses are also called standardbreds. Standardbreds are a close cousin to the thoroughbred since all registered American harness and thoroughbred horses can trace their ancestry to the same founding fathers. Standardbreds, however, are much sturdier animals and have been cross-bred with other horses. The inbreeding in thoroughbreds has produced a faster but less sound animal. Standardbreds thrive on work; even on race day a horse will be trotted or paced several miles to keep the horse in racing trim.

About 80 percent of all harness races are between pacers. The pacer has a peculiar gait aided by the presence of hopples connected to each leg. Hopples are straps that prevent the horse from breaking into a run and thus keep the horse pacing. A pacer's front legs will move in step with his back legs. As he throws his right front out, the hopple forces the right hind leg forward with it. Then he throws the left front out and the hopple forces the left back leg forward. This left side-right side gait is called pacing. Not all pacers use hobbling equipment to force the horse into this irregular gait, but all pacers must maintain this gait throughout the race.

The trotters do not use this hobbling equipment and their gait is different. The trotter throws out his left front and his right hind leg, then the next step is right front with left hind. A horse running at full gallop will not pay attention to which leg goes where; the run will be much smoother, his legs fairly straight much of the time. If asked for speed, a horse will naturally run at a gallop, not a trot or a pace. Since the harness horse, however, is unable to run with a smooth stride, his front knees will be constantly rising up in a pumping motion in order to gain more speed.

Frequently a harness horse will be unable to confine the gait and will break into galloping. A horse is not allowed to gain ground while galloping, and the rules of harness racing are that a driver must pull the horse out of the way of other horses when his horse breaks the gait. Then, if the driver can get the horse back into the proper gait, the horse can rejoin the race.

Usually a horse is completely eliminated by a break. The hopples prevent most pacers from breaking gait. Horses will break for the following reasons: interference from other horses; the horse is trying to move too fast; the horse is tired; an essential piece of equipment, such as the hopple, breaks; the horse hits one leg against another; or the horse starts the race off stride. This tendency to break is a major factor in handicapping harness racing, whether trotters or pacers. While the pacers' hopples prevent the horse from galloping, they do not prevent the horse from trying to break, thus throwing it off-stride. Breaking is one element in harness racing missing in thoroughbred handicapping. The other major factors have thoroughbred equivalents. The other six prominent factors in handicapping harness racing are: current condition, class, speed, track biases, post position, and driver. Harness tracks come in three basic sizes: half mile, five furlong, and one mile. At the one-mile tracks, the post position factor is eliminated, leaving a bare minimum of factors that can determine the outcome of a race.

The racing programs at each track will provide most of the information necessary concerning all these factors. How to read the standard harness racing program is shown in the illustration on page 14. A brief rundown on the importance of each major handicapping factor follows.

Speed

Speed is the paramount factor in handicapping trotters and pacers. The trotting and pacing gaits put an unusual demand upon a horse; each horse, when it is in top condition, seems to hit a maximum speed. If the horse is pushed to go faster, it will break or tire. Each horse's best winning time plus the times of its most recent races will be listed in the program. Since virtually all races are at one mile, it is easy to compare the best recent times of each horse. A horse which is consistently faster than the other horses, providing it is not eliminated by post position, condition, driver, or tendency to break, will likely win. This will be true at any harness track, in either type of race. The fastest horse will win as long as it is not eliminated by one of the other major factors. The fastest horse often wins even when it is hampered by poor post position, bad driver, or breaking tendencies, but it is best not to bet such a horse. Bet the fastest horse in the race as long as no more than one of these three factors is present. Never, never bet any horse that is not in condition.

Also note the fractional times of the most recent races of each horse. If the half mile was unusually fast or unusually slow, this could provide a horse with an excuse for doing poorly in its last race. Expect a late-racing horse to do poorly if the half was extra slow. Expect an early-speed horse to do poorly if the half was exceedingly fast.

Current Condition

Sharp animals win; tired or stale horses lose. This is true in any type of racing. Current condition is readily apparent in harness racing. Most trotters and pacers race every week to ten days. A layoff of three weeks or more is immediately suspect. A longer layoff because of injury or illness requires the horse to race in a qualifying race before being allowed back to betting races. If a horse's last race was a qualifying race, eliminate him if his final time was not close to or better than the most recent times of the other animals the horse faces in his present race. Eliminate a horse that has been laid off two weeks or more (unless it is a high-class stakes horse). Eliminate any horse that lost ground in the stretch of his last race yet did not flash any speed in the early stages of the race. A horse in this condition would show this type of entry for his last performance:

$$5 \quad 5 \quad 5 \quad 5 \quad 7^7$$

Also eliminate a horse (as long as it is not going down in class) if it was just carried along in its last race, even if it finished close up. This horse might show the following entry for its last performance:

$$3 \quad 3 \quad 3 \quad 3 \quad 3^2$$

41

Neither horse has made a move in its last race; to be considered in condition, a horse has to show some sign of life in its last race or have a legitimate excuse for not doing well. Excuses include equipment breaks, interference, sloppy or muddy track, bad driver, bad post position, higher class. It must be noted here that in most harness races there is a great deal of single-file trotting or pacing. A horse in an inside post can grab the rail easily and hold it throughout the race without ever making another move. If the horse is lucky, the other horses will knock each other out and this horse could win or at least finish in the money. But, make no mistake about it. The result of the race is not up to this horse; it will only benefit from the mistakes or misfortunes of others and is just as likely to finish last as first. If a horse did not make a move in its last race, barring excuses, no matter where the horse finished, it is not likely to be in condition for its next race.

A good sign of superior condition is if a horse raced well despite being on the outside during the running of a race. Since the harness horse pulls a bike, if it races on the outside of horses, it races several yards from the rail, losing ground with every step. In the racing program, it is recorded if a horse races outside for at least one-quarter mile. By taking this longer route a horse can easily tire. Being parked outside also implies a battle between other horses to get the coveted rail position. Watch out particularly for a horse that was parked out in its last race when starting in an outside position, which now gets a more favorable inside position. If the horse raced well despite a disadvantageous post, it should do better on the inside.

Harness horses do not have published workouts, but instead work out on race day before the night's races begin. Come to the track early and note which horses are trotting or pacing stiffly or laboriously. The horses will be labeled by number and saddle cloth color for each race so you will know which horse is which. Also watch before the race to see if any horse looks dull or droopy, or if any horse looks extra chipper. The program does not tell everything about a horse's current condition; how he feels the night of the race is reflected in his personal appearance.

Post Position

Even casual harness racing bettors are aware of the post position biases of most tracks. Tracks publish statistics on the numbers of starters winning at each post position. And year after year the same patterns prevail. At the half-mile tracks, the first three post positions win the lion's share of races; the outer two posts are constant losers. At the five-furlong tracks the difference is still there, but not quite as marked. And at the mile tracks, post position importance fades.

The reasons for these post position biases are simple. At the half-mile tracks, the start is near the first turn; there are four sharp turns in all. An outside horse has to show excessive early speed to get into good position on that first turn. What will likely happen is that an inside horse will grab the rail and force that outside horse to remain parked out for much of the race, losing ground and strength with every step. With sharp turns early position is essential. It is impossible to gain ground on the turns; the straightaways on a half-mile track are too short for a horse to rally unless he is up close. At the five-furlong distance, the bias is lessened; the race starts in the backstretch with more running room to the first turn. Yet the inside horses still face less danger of being parked out; the outer horses still must show early speed to jockey for position. But both the stretch and backstretch are longer, allowing for

43

greater rallying room.

At the mile tracks, there is little post-position bias; more room to maneuver for outside horses means less of an advantage to inside horses. Since most harness racing is now run at half-mile tracks, however, post position is an important consideration. Eliminate any horse from the seventh or eighth (or beyond) post, unless the horse has raced significantly faster than all the other contenders in the race and has a superior driver. If there are two contenders of seemingly equal class, condition, and driver, favor the inside horse, as long as the post difference is four positions or more. (Favor Post 2 over Post 6, for example.)

Track Biases and Condition

Like post position, track bias and condition are related to the size of the track. The half-mile tracks place a premium on early speed. These horses get in good racing position and tend to hold on better because of the lack of rallying room for late-racing horses. This premium is less pronounced at five-furlong tracks and the tendency is reversed at mile tracks. At mile tracks, early-speed horses fade and come-from-behind horses do better. A horse that usually fades on a five-furlong track will do better on a half-mile track. Eliminate faders going to mile tracks. Eliminate late-running horses going from five-furlong or mile tracks to half-milers. (Only eliminate a horse if it goes up from or stays in the equivalent class.)

Track conditions range from fast to sloppy, good, slow, heavy, or muddy. Try to avoid off-tracks in harness racing. It introduces an element of doubt in every race. Each harness track reacts differently in mud. Some tracks also run thoroughbred meetings; others are exclusively for trotters. The track surfaces are drastically different. Windsor Raceway in Canada has a tartan, artificial surface, for instance. Hazel Park, across the river near Detroit, is sand. The horses in the Detroit circuit frequently go from Windsor to Hazel Park and vice versa. But there is no way of determining how a Windsor horse will react to Hazel Park mud or how a Hazel Park horse will react to a watery Windsor track. Avoid any race on an off-track unless every horse in the race has had a race on this current track in its current condition.

Class

Class is a confusing element in harness handicapping. Tracks have conditioned, classified, claiming, and preferred racing. Not all tracks have all types of racing; horses in one group can race in another, and the class of any particular horse may not be readily apparent by the track program's past performances. In classified racing, horses race in the following classes, from lowest to highest: D, C-3, C-2, C-1, B-3, B-2, B-1, A-3, A-2, A-1, AA, Junior free for all (JFA), Free for all (FFA). Horses race according to where the track secretary feels they belong.

Classified racing in many states has given way to conditioned racing. A conditioned race is similar to a thoroughbred allowance race. Horses are eligible for the race if they meet the conditions. A sample race might be for nonwinners of $2000 in 1975; or nonwinners of $10,000 (lifetime).

Track secretaries also provide claiming races for the cheaper stock at each track. Claiming races are assigned a price and each horse entered can be bought (or claimed) at that price. The claiming race is enjoying increased popularity at American harness racing tracks because it does provide racing opportunities for lesser trotters and pacers. The final category is preferred; these races include junior free for all, free for all, and stakes races. These races are for the best animals at the track; the class divisions are fairly clear here. But among condition, classified, and claiming horses, there are no clear delineations. A horse might run in B-1 one week, in a nonwinners of $5000 another week, and a $7500 claimer the week after. The only way to tell which race is classiest is to keep a record of purses and conditions of all the races at your track. This entails a small investment of buying the track program every day, whether or not you intend to go to the track. Harness racing programs are available at the same newsstands that carry the *Daily Racing Form*. The records are essential. To tell relative class you must know what competition a horse has been running against. The program does not carry all this information. For example, if the two top contenders in a race are inseparable according to condition, driver, post position, and other essential factors, and both horses have been in conditioned races with purses at $5000, this is reflected in the program entry as Cd 5000. But one race was for older horses, nonwinners of $12,000 this year. The other was for three year olds, nonwinners of $10,000 lifetime. The former horse faced tougher competition, but the program does not indicate this. Your records should.

Age and Sex

Age and sex are related to class. Unlike thoroughbred racing, fillies and mares can regularly beat male horses. For some reason, female pacers are, as a rule, not as good as male pacers, yet are at the top in the trotting field. Do not discount a filly or a mare in any trot or pace if it has raced well in the curent class. Standardbreds reach full maturity after the age of four. Do not bet a younger horse against older ones unless the older horses are cheap and the younger horse's best time is one full second faster than the recent best times of the other contenders. Good younger horses are sometimes eligible for cheap races; but it is essential to determine their ability by speed differences before betting on them against older horses.

Driver

The driver in harness racing plays a greater part than the jockey in thoroughbred racing. For one thing, the driver is usually also the trainer of the horse and as often as not the owner as well, so the driver should know the horse thoroughly. The driver has to get the horse going as fast as possible without bumping into other horses and without pushing the horse so hard that the animal breaks gait. At the end of many harness races, it will look as if the driver is holding back the horse by pulling on the reins. Usually, however, he is trying to keep the tiring animal from breaking while maintaining maximum speed.

Drivers have, of late, acquired a very poor reputation. Fixes and rumors of fixes have hit harness racing with astounding regularity. There will be no denials of dishonesty here. But the manner of fixing is less obvious than pulling back on the reins at the finish line. At the standard half-mile track if a horse does not begin its move at the start of the second half mile, it will likely lose. A driver simply has to keep his horse tucked in until the middle of the backstretch. Then, finding no room, he legitimately loses the race. Or a driver can send his horse out front in a killing race, looking dumb but honest as the horse fades in the stretch. It is so easy to fix a harness race, there is no reason to be obvious about it. There is reason, however, for the bettor to be worried about it. If a driver can make more money by losing a race than by winning, he may throw the race. The profit in fixing races lies in those exotic bets popularized by the harness tracks. In exotic betting, the right $2 can win thousands; certain drivers will try to get in on those payoffs by pulling horses.

It is suggested that the racing fan avoid favorites in triples or other exotic bets. Particularly avoid favorites if driven by people who have been previously involved in betting scandals. The bigger exotic payoffs are achieved by keeping the favorite, or other low-odds horses, out of the money. In general, however, favor any horse who is driven by one of the top drivers locally or nationally. Eliminate a contender with a bad driver unless the horse has an inside post position and is significantly faster than any horse in the race. If the best horse in the race has an outside post position, but a good driver, bet him. Conditions are not optimum, but the driver should overcome the post position problem.

Tendency to Break

Avoid any horse with a tendency to break. This does not include horses that have broken recently because of equipment problems or interferences; just those horses who have broken gait in two of the last five races. Avoid any race in which two or more horses are breakers, unless your horse has the extreme inside or extreme outside post. Breakers can eliminate more than themselves in a race. If your horse is far enough away from potential breakers, do not worry. But in most situations, your horse could be affected by those breakers.

Betting

The likely winner of a race is the fastest animal not eliminated by any of the other factors. If the horse has a good post position and a good driver, bet it if the odds are 2-1 or higher. If the horse is hampered by post position or driver, only bet it if the odds are 3-1 or higher. In the latter instance, luck will have a greater play in the outcome since the horse has to overcome a disadvantage. The higher odds will cover that disadvantage and allow an edge. These odds rules should provide you with overlays as long as you do not bet any horse or any race in which there are serious questions. Only bet if there are sufficient past performances showing the relative abilities of each contender. When betting on harness racing, adhere to these following rules.

1. Only bet on races in which each of the contenders has had a recent race on this track.
2. Always bet win and place; bet show if the horse is 8-1 or better.
3. Do not bet below 2-1; pass up the race if the best horse goes below 2-1. If there are two contenders, bet both if their odds are above 3-1.
4. Eliminate any race in which two or more of the horses had less than five races, lifetime.
5. Avoid any race in which the class of a horse in condition is unclear.
6. Keep records of the purses and conditions of all races at your track.
7. Avoid races on off-tracks.
8. Eliminate a horse that lost ground in the stretch in its last race if it did not show some early speed, or was parked out, or is going down in class.
9. Do not bet a chronic breaker.
10. Eliminate horses in outside post positions at half-mile tracks unless the driver and horse are obviously superior.

11. Bet the fastest horse in the race unless it is eliminated by another factor.
12. Eliminate any horse, on grounds of condition, that did not flash any signs of life in its last race or did not have any excuses for failure to do so. Do not bet any out of condition horses.
13. Do not bet away from the track; always watch the horses in person before making a bet.
14. Avoid triples, exactas, and other exotic bets. Avoid favorites in these races.
15. Do not bet on a poor driver unless the horse has all the other factors going for it.
16. Do not bet your whole bankroll on one horse.
17. Do not bet more than you can afford to lose.

2

Card Games

Poker, blackjack, and gin rummy reign as the basic American gambling card games. Other games such as bridge or hearts sometimes include betting, but it is not necessarily an essential element. In this chapter only those games which have become an integral part of the gambling scene will be discussed: poker and all its major variations; blackjack and its cousins, chemin de fer and baccarat; and gin rummy.

Poker is the pre-eminent gambling card game; more fortunes have been won and lost on this one game than all the other gambling opportunities combined. Blackjack now rivals craps as the most popular casino game. And gin rummy is played in clubs and homes for both high and low stakes across the United States. Each game is beatable by the smart player because each requires skill to win.

The following sections describe how to play, gamble, and win consistently at draw poker, stud poker, low ball poker, high-low poker, three-card monte, hold 'em, casino blackjack, private blackjack, baccarat, chemin de fer, and gin rummy.

POKER

Poker is impossible to play without gambling. The raises, bluffs, and showdowns are what the game is all about. It may be the most popular game in America; everyone plays it sooner or later (this writer learned at the age of six). Yet it is often misunderstood. The most common misconception is that if you have the right cards, you will win. Keep thinking that and you may lose the deed to the farm one day. Poker is instead a game of skill. Getting good cards helps, but it will not necessarily make you a winner; knowing your opponents, knowing when to fold, and knowing the chances of winning on any particular hand will.

First, the basic rules for playing winning poker:

1. *Never play with strangers.* It is not all that difficult to cheat somebody in a card game. Card mechanics are a dime a dozen, and if you are alone among strangers, you may be in for a fleecing. Even if the strangers do not appear to know each other or even seem antagonistic, do not trust appearances. This writer knows someone who runs an illicit card game in Michigan and sucks in the fish by putting on a fake fight between him and his mechanic. The sucker thinks the game operator hates this other player and feels safe from any two-way cheating, until he starts losing steadily and the smiles start passing between the supposed enemies. If you ever do get in a game with strangers, get out as soon as you find yourself losing steadily. They may not be cheating, but it is bad practice to continue the game. You should also remember that an essential part of poker is assessing your opponents and being able to predict when they have the cards or are merely bluffing. If you do not know anything about the other players, it is hard to gauge their reactions. Nick

Zographos, the leader of a syndicate of gamblers that won millions a few decades ago, had this advice for poker players: "Keep close track of how much money every opponent you face has lost, and make it your business to know how much he can afford to lose. The information is vital and should influence your style of play. When a player is under heavy financial pressure and you know it, his betting can almost tell you what cards he's holding." Playing with strangers becomes too much of a guessing game. Even if your opponents are only casual acquaintances, you are better off than playing against someone you know nothing about.

2. *Never play over your head.* Whether the stakes are too high or the other players are too good, you are bound to lose. If the stakes are too high, you will always be betting more than you can afford to lose. You stand to get hurt on any hand, and this can drastically affect your style of play. You may constantly get shut out of the pots because you cannot keep up with the betting. A normally strong player may get so far behind that he starts playing carelessly in order to win back the money he has already lost. Or, as often happens, the player will lose his nerve and get bluffed out of far too many winning hands because he cannot stand a substantial loss. The result is the same in any case; the player will eventually lose because he is at the mercy of the other players. A weaker player is also at the mercy of the other players. They are eventually going to grind him down. In a game with good poker players, it is often the case that the better players all wind up winners at the end of an evening, while one poor sucker, who just was not good enough but had enough money to keep him in the game for hours, is the big loser. In fact, professional poker players seem to make most of their money in this type of situation. They will take turns beating each other, while waiting for a free-spending fish who thinks he can

play poker.

3. *"Don't play 'em unless you got 'em."*—Damon Runyon. If you stick around on every hand of stud or draw, just to see what final cards you will be dealt, you will surely lose. Drop out of a hand early unless you have a fair chance of winning or the betting is light enough so far to continue your presence in the hand. A strong poker player plays the percentages, but only on solid cards, and that means not playing out every hand. Even in a bluffing situation, the good poker player does not continue unless he has something and a reasonable promise of something better. More about this later. In stud poker this means folding after the third card is dealt; in draw this means folding before the draw unless you have good cards.

4. *Drop out of hands on variations in which you are not sure of the rules or winning percentages.* Low ball and high-low are very popular with big-time gamblers, but they can be very confusing to the casual bettor. Flushes and straights do not count in determining low hands and aces are low. You may know the percentages of drawing to a full house when you have two pair, but can you figure the odds on drawing to nothing after discarding a king? Some of these situations will be covered in this chapter, but it is wise not to play a game like this for significant stakes until you are experienced at it. Likewise, try to avoid games in which the dealers keep calling wild cards every hand. Poker is supposed to be a game of skill and percentage. Wild cards reduce the skill, play havoc with the percentages, and increase the element of pure chance. A few games of wild card will not matter, but too many, and your playing will get sloppy.

5. *Do not bet unless the payoff is at least equal to the odds against your winning.* Fold if the odds do not justify your continued play. Take, for instance, a hand in draw in

which you have been dealt five cards. Four of these are hearts and one is an unrepentant spade. There are forty-seven cards you have not seen. Nine of these cards are hearts and will help you. The other thirty-eight are of no use. If you discard that spade and draw, you have a 38-9 chance of hitting a heart flush or 9-2 against. You have a chance of betting or folding before the draw. The bet is $2 to stay in; the pot has $16 in it. Since you stand to receive $18 for a $2 investment, the payoff is 8-1. According to the law of averages, you will hit this flush twice out of every time nine times you draw that fifth card (based on hundreds or thousands of plays). To break even on this bet, you need a payoff of $9 plus your $2 investment. With this 8-1 promised payoff, the odds are considerably on your side. Make the bet and draw the final card. Conversely, if the pot is $16 and the bet $5, the payoff is now 3-1, but the chances of hitting remain the same. Fold.

6. *Do not be afraid of being bluffed. Do not be afraid of bluffing yourself. Do not be afraid of being caught while bluffing.* Bluffing is a big part of the game, but do not let the prospect of being bluffed throw you. Some players think poker is a test of courage. They feel spineless when someone bluffs them out of a hand (though good poker players do not tell when they have just won by bluff) and live in mortal fear of being considered weak by the other players in the game. Gambling of any sort is a poor and ultimately costly way of testing courage. Certainly the risk involved is what makes it a thrill for most players; a poker player who lacks nerve will get wiped out quickly. But a good gambler at poker, or any other game, takes only calculated risks. His betting is determined by the chances he has of winning plus his assessment of the other players. Particularly if he is playing against strong players, he folds if he does not have the cards. Foolish

risks will not win in the long run. Drop out whenever the odds are not in your favor. If you play only reasonably strong hands and with the percentages, an occasional bluff out will not matter; you will still win regularly.

While the wise course is to play only strong hands, do not be afraid of bluffing. After playing against someone for awhile you may be able to tell when they can be bluffed—their weaknesses and strengths will determine this. A weak player may be bluffed only when he has completely lost his nerve because of heavy financial losses. If he is not losing, it may be harder because too often the weak player plays wildly and does not know when to drop out. He is so afraid of being bluffed he will never fold. A better player, however, can often be bluffed because he will not play a weak hand too far. But a word of warning: do not go into a hand intending to bluff your way to the pot. Bluff only after you have stayed in the betting on the reasonable expectations that your hand would improve enough for a clear win, but the hand did not pan out. By staying and upping your bets, you may be able to convince your opponents that your hand did improve in the desired manner.

In the early stages of the game particularly, you should try to get caught bluffing at least once. But make that losing pot a small one. During the first couple of hours, players try to figure out their opponents' methods of play and personalities. If you get caught early in a bluff, certain players will mark you as a bluffer and nothing will change their minds, not even hours of straight play. Since you will primarily play only strong hands, these players will constantly stay in with you, trying to call your bluff while building your winning pots, when they should be folding.

7. *Do not throw good money after bad.* If the betting on a particular hand is getting too steep for the cards you

hold, do not fall victim to the "I've gone this far, I might as well stick it out to the end" thinking. There may be no limit to how high the betting will go; save your money for another, stronger hand. Likewise, if the whole evening is starting to prove costly, do not keep trying to win back your losses. If you are losing steadily, your game is off, and by pushing you will only lose more. Go home.

With those basic guidelines in mind following is how to play and win at the most popular forms of poker.

Draw Poker

In standard draw poker each player is dealt five cards face down, one at a time. Before the deal, each player puts a small amount of money in the pot, called the ante. After the initial deal, there is a betting interval, after which the players who have not folded draw new cards from the deck, first discarding those cards deemed unhelpful in making a winning hand. Following the draw, there is another betting interval ended by a showdown. The winner is the player with the best hand who has not previously withdrawn from the betting. In descending order, the winning hands at the showdown are:

Royal Flush: Ace, king, queen, jack, and 10 of one suit (clubs, spades, hearts, or diamonds). Suits have no intrinsic value; if two players have royal flushes, they split the pot.

Straight Flush: Five cards of one suit in consecutive order such as 7, 8, 9, 10, and jack of clubs. If two or more players have straight flushes, the winner is the player whose straight begins with the highest card.

Four of a Kind: Four of the same cards, such as four kings, four threes, etc. If two or more players have four of a kind, highest card wins. For example four kings beat four threes.

Full House: Three cards of one denomination plus two cards of another, such as three kings and two nines. In situations in which two players hold full houses, the winner is the player whose three of a kind card is higher. Three kings and two deuces will beat three jacks and two deuces.

Flush: Five cards of one suit, in no particular order, such as 10, 8, 3, 2, and 6 of clubs. If two or more players hold flushes, the winner is the player with the highest card. For example, A, 10, 8, 7, and 3 of clubs beat king, jack, queen, 9, and 6 of hearts, etc.

Straight: Five cards in consecutive order, of no particular suit, such as 10 of diamonds, 9 of clubs, 8 of diamonds, 7 of spades, 6 of hearts. If two or more players hold straights, the winner is the player whose straights start with the highest card.

Three of a kind: Three cards of one denomination, such as three kings, three sevens, etc. Three kings beat three sevens.

Two Pairs: Two cards of one denomination, plus two cards of another denomination, such as two eights and two sixes. If two or more players have two pairs, the player with the highest pair wins; kings and eights beat queens and jacks.

One Pair: Two cards of one denomination, such as two aces. The high pair wins, for example, two aces beat two kings.

High Card: When all players have no pairs, straights, or flushes, the player with the highest card wins. For example, ace high beats king high; king high beats queen high; ace, king beats ace, queen; ace, king, 8 beats ace, king, 7, etc.

These hands apply to all variations of draw and stud

poker except low ball. Low-ball hands will be explained later.

There are two basic forms of draw poker: jackpots and open.

Jackpots. In jackpots, a player can only open the betting if he has a pair of jacks or better. If no player has high enough opening cards, the hand is folded. The players then ante again for the next deal. In progressive jackpots, on the next hand, openers must be queens or better. If no player holds these cards, the hand is folded again and the next deal requires a pair of kings or better to open.

Only the opener has to have a pair of jacks or better to open in jackpots. The other players can bet and stay in on anything. A player without the required openers can pass when the opening question gets to him and then get in after another player opens the betting. In open draw, anything and anyone can open the betting. In both games only those players who bet or meet the other players' bets, are allowed to draw cards. The others fold.

In jackpots, it is usually a matter of honor whether a player actually has jacks or better when opening. But if a player gets to the showdown and it is apparent that he did not have the required cards, his winnings on that hand will be forfeited. He will also be marked as both dishonest and stupid by his fellow poker players.

In jackpots it is a stupid move to open the betting on less than a pair of jacks; even if you win, you will lose the pot and it is highly unlikely that you will win.It is also unwise to stay in a hand of jackpots with less than a pair of jacks; if you cannot beat that or at least match it before the draw, you should fold. You have no assurances that your hand will improve. So far it is a loser. Unless the probable payoff exceeds the chances for improvement, drop before the draw. To explain further, following are a few sample hands of jackpot poker.

There are six players including yourself and the dealer. The player to the dealer's left has the first chance to open the betting, then the player to his left and so on until the opportunity hits the dealer. You are on the dealer's right throughout this series of plays. (Betting and ante amounts are strictly arbitrary and are used only to calculate the odds on hitting certain hands.)

Jackpot Hand #1

Each player antes $1 for an initial pot of $6. The cards are dealt and the first two players pass. Thus you know they do not have jacks or better. The third player bets $2; the fourth player sees or meets this bet. The decision is now yours. There is $10 in the pot; you have to invest $2 to stay in. Your cards are 9, 9, 10, and 3. You have a pair of nines, but the third player already has you beat. The fourth player might also beat a pair of nines. Fold. You may improve, but player three has the same chance of improving. You will be relying on luck if you stay in. And remember, the sensible gambler does not rely on luck.

Jackpot Hand #2

Again each player antes $1. Your cards are A, A, J, 10, and 9. The first player opens with a $2 bet. The second player folds. The third player sees the $2 bet. The fourth player folds. It is your turn again. The likelihood is that both players have jacks or better. The third player, however, probably does not have much over that or he would have raised the bet. You should raise. Try to drive as many other players out as possible. You have good opening cards, a chance of hitting three of a kind, a full house, or two pairs. (The odds against two pairs are 5-1, three of a kind 8-1, full house 97-1. For a full description of the odds on drawing any particular hand, see the chart on page 75.)

But the other players also have that same chance. You can assume that your pair of aces, up to now, beats the third player. But it is best to get him out before he lucks into a better hand. So you see the $2 bet and raise another $2. The dealer folds. The first player sees your raise. The third player, believing you to have a better hand than his, folds. There is now $16 in the pot. Both remaining players draw. The first player draws one card, you draw three. Since it is jacks or better, it is apparent that the other player had two pairs on the initial deal. He could not be going for a straight or a flush because four-card straights or flushes cannot be used as openers. It is also apparent to the other player that you have one pair, probably aces or kings, or you would not have raised or stayed on less.

After the draw, the first player reopens the betting. He bets $2. This low opening can mean one of two things. He did not get the necessary cards to turn those two pairs into a full house, or he has made his hand and he is trying to suck you in. On the draw, your hand improved to A, A, K, K, and 8. Before the draw your opponent had you beat. Two pairs always beat one pair. After the draw to two high pairs, the odds have shifted to your favor. He needs a full house to beat you. The odds against his having drawn a full house are 11-1, so the odds are significantly against his having improved well enough to beat you. (If he did not hit the full house, your aces and kings will likely beat his two-pair hand, unless he has the identical two pairs, and a single card higher than eight. This will not happen often enough to worry about.)

Do not worry about your opponent's strategy; raise his bet, and raise it big. According to the law of averages, you have the cards. He will hit that full house on one out of every twelve chances. Two high pairs will win the remaining eleven plays. (Since your odds on hitting the two pair were 5-1 and his chances were 11-1 against, it might be assumed that this gives you only a two out of three advantage over your opponent. However, what you draw has no effect either on your opponent's chances of hitting the full house or on your odds of beating him after you have drawn the two pairs. Once you have two pairs, he can only beat you with a full house; it is 11-1 against that, thus, you can confidently raise.

Jackpots #3

Everyone antes $1. The first player opens for $2. The second player sees the bet. The third player folds. The fourth player also sees the bet, but does not raise. There is $12 now in the pot. It will cost you $2 to stay in; $12 to $2 means 6-1 odds. Your cards are A, 10, 9, 8, and 7 or a four-card straight. There are eight cards that can help you—four jacks and four sixes. There are fifty-two cards in the deck; you have seen five, leaving forty-seven. Eight of those forty-seven can help for a 5-1 proposition. The 6-1 pot is worth the 5-1 risk since it offers you an edge. However, had that fourth player raised the bet, say $4, the pot would be $16, but you would have to bet $6 to stay in (the $2 original bet plus the raise). In this case, you fold.

In general, in jackpots never stay in with less than a pair of kings. The opener has at least a pair of jacks; staying with queens cuts it a bit close and too often results in a losing hand. In the betting interval before the draw, each player in succession has a chance of opening the betting. But if player one does not have the required openers, he does not have to fold. He can simply pass, waiting for another player to open the betting, then after all the other players have made their betting decisions, can also stay in. This is, of course, not usually a recommended course. He has already announced the inadequacy of his hand by not being able to open the betting. He should only stay in this situation if he has a four-card straight or flush, and then should get out unless the bet is low enough and the payoff high enough to give him an edge.

Never stay on a three-card straight. If you have reasonable staying and opening cards such as a high pair or a low three of a kind, try to force out as many other players from the draw as possible. That player with a pair of jacks will beat your three fours if he is lucky in the draw. Do not let him stay that far; convince him you have tough cards to beat.

Open Draw. In open draw, much of the playing advice is the same. A player can open with anything, but it is simply unwise to open with less than a pair of kings. Jackpots gives you a slightly better idea of what your opponents' cards are or should be. Until proven otherwise, assume that players will not open or bet with rotten cards, and drop out before the draw unless your cards are fairly good. The following are a few sample hands of open draw.

Open Hand #1

You are now the fourth player in a six-player game. Everyone still antes $1. Player one opens with $2, player two sees and raises another $3. Player three sees players one and two. There is $18 in the pot and your bet has to be $5. Players have a greater tendency to stay in and see in open draw because there is no opening requirement. Thus the greater action. Your hand is 9, 9, 6, 7, and 3—rotten cards. You fold.

If in the same betting situation, your cards were 8, 8, 7, 7, and 4, you should also fold. Two small pairs will rarely win at draw. You have to assume that one or more of those three players have a pair of jacks or better, maybe even three of a kind. Drawing to three of a kind from one pair is 8-1 chance; drawing to two pairs—the top one of which will beat your eights—is only 5-1. For you to improve you need a full house. It is 11-1 against that; the pot is $18 and your bet is $5 for a lousy proposition. Fold.

Again, the same betting situation, but you are dealt A, A, 10, 9, 8. If only one or two players had stayed in, you might raise to knock them out, but as of now, your two aces looks a bit small for that. Do not fold, however; your odds of improving are good enough, and a pair of aces is a good opening hand in draw poker.

Open Hand #2

Everyone antes $1. You are now the second player. Player one opens at $2. Your cards are 10, 9, 8, 7, 6—a small straight. You would like as many players to stay in as possible, so you mere see the bet. If you were the fifth or sixth to bet and several players had already stayed in, then by all means, you should raise. But a straight, a flush, or a full house is a strong hand and will usually win in draw poker. Someone might luck out and beat you. But remember there are 2.5 million possible poker hands in a fifty-two card deck. A straight will beat all but nine thousand of those hands. The odds are way in your favor. If the betting gets back to you before the draw, raise then. Needless to say, you do not draw any cards. This is a tip-off to the other players that you have a full hand. Make an average size bet so you do not scare the suckers away or limit your eventual winning pot too much.

Open Hand #3

You are the fourth player again. All six players ante. The first player opens for $2. The second sees his $2 bet, the third raises it $3. The pot is now $15. Your bet is $5. Your cards are 4, 4, 4, 7, and 8. You make a substantial raise, say $10. This will drive out several of those players and prevent them from staying in the draw. If you draw two cards, it is a 15½-1 shot that you will hit a full house, and only one card (that last four) can give you four of a kind. So you might not want to draw at all. By not drawing, it will appear that you have a full hand—a straight, flush, or full house. Your chances of winning by convincing your fellow players that you have a full hand may be significantly greater than your chances of drawing a better hand—in this case, a full house or four of a kind.

What you do in this situation will be determined by your assessment of the other players who stay in after your original raise. In this example, the dealer and player one met your raise. Player one, a good poker player, would not have met your raise if he did not have good cards. He discarded one card which means he has either two pairs, a four-card straight, a four-card flush, or possibly four of a kind. The latter situation is unlikely and happens too rarely for you to worry about. Since he is a strong player, he probably has two pairs or he would not have met your $10 raise on hopes to hit a flush or straight. You have him beat so far, and it is 11-1 against his making a full house.

You are a little more worried about the dealer. He met the original $15 bet with little trepidation, meaning he probably has good cards. But, he has been losing all night and he cannot afford more losses. Your three fours may not beat him in a showdown; your chances of improving are worse than player one's. The way to beat the dealer then is to get him to chicken out. So you do not draw any cards. The dealer draws two. You know he has three if a kind; nobody is stupid enough to draw to a three-card flush or straight. The dealer has you beat before the draw. But psychologically you have the dealer beat. Player one bets lightly, indicating he did not full his hand and he fears your cards. You bet big. The dealer folds. You win the pot.

This is all based on your observations of your fellow players. If the dealer is not in financial trouble, do not try to bluff him by not drawing. Draw and take your chances. But remember that a psychological advantage can sometimes beat good cards.

In open draw poker the admonitions are the same, drop out before the draw unless you have kings or better. Only stay in if the potential payoff justifies the risk.

Stud Poker

There are two basic variations of stud poker: seven card and five card. There is no ante at the beginning. In five-card stud, five cards are dealt, the first face down, the final four face up. There is a betting interval following the deal of the second, third, fourth, and fifth cards. In seven-card stud the first two cards are dealt face down, the next four face up, and the final card face down. There is a betting interval following the deal of the third, fourth, fifth, sixth, and seventh cards. A player can drop out during any of the betting intervals. The winning hands are the same as those in draw poker; in seven-card stud the best five of the seven cards dealt is considered the hand. In both games the opening bettor in any round is the player who has the best hand or highest card showing. If in five-card stud, for example, after the first exposed card is dealt to each player, one player has an ace, another a jack, and another a ten—the ace opens. If two players were dealt aces, the player who was dealt the first ace opens.

In both stud games, as in draw, it is best to get out quickly unless you have reasonable cards. In five-card stud the first decision to drop comes after the second card is dealt. Drop unless both cards are above ten, unless your hole (unexposed) card is an ace or a king. If you have a small pair, say eights, and no one so far shows a card above eight, stay for the third card. On the third card, the same rule applies; stay only on higher cards or if your small pair is not visibly beaten. Stay, of course, if you have hit three of a kind. Consider if your hole card is a jack, and you have a king and ten showing. If another player has two aces showing, he has you beat. The only way you can beat him is by drawing two more cards to a straight, or two pairs, or possibly three of a kind. Drop out. The cards look nice, but they are losers. The following are two sample five-card stud games.

Five-Card Stud #1

On round one all six players are dealt one card face down; round two the cards are face up. You are the fourth player, your hole card is an ace. This is what the total deal so far looks like to you:

Player 1	?	J
Player 2	?	10
Player 3	?	7
Player 4	A	Q
Player 5	?	A
Player 6	?	3

Player five opens since his ace is high; player six folds; player one raises slightly, player two sees the initial bet and raises, player three folds. You also see player five's bet and player one's raise. The third round looks like this:

Player 1	?	J	9
Player 2	?	10	10
Player 4	A	Q	A
Player 5	?	A	3

The pair of tens bets; you raise slightly; player five and player one also stay in for the fourth round, which develops this way:

Player 1	?	J	9	10
Player 2	?	10	10	A
Player 4	A	Q	A	Q
Player 5	?	A	3	10

You are now high and you have everyone beat so far. Player five cannot have a pair of aces because you hold two and player two holds the other. Player two cannot have three tens since both player one and player five have tens showing. The most player one can have is a pair of jacks. Since he raised back in round two, that is probably what he does have. Few players raise on a two-card straight. So the decision is whether to bet lightly to keep some of those sure losers in awhile longer, or to bet big to either win immediately or force out the potential winners. Do not take chances. The pot is yours now. Get those other players out. Player one, if he does have a pair of jacks, can beat you with three of a kind. Or if he is trying for a straight, he could make it. Player two cannot beat you no matter what he draws, but player five could beat you if his hole card is a three and he draws another one in the final round. By betting big, you can force out player one; the others may be stupid enough to stay in further. Certainly player five should have dropped out as soon as he got that three.

In this example you do bet big and all three players drop out, leaving you the pot. You might have manipulated it into a larger sum, but do that only when you are sure that a final round cannot hurt you, or when you are not sure you have them beat on round four.

Five-Card Stud #2

After the second card is dealt, the cards look like this to you, the fourth player:

Player 1	?	A
Player 2	?	J
Player 3	?	3
Player 4	2	K
Player 5	?	J
Player 6	?	7

You are beat already so drop out. You may get a second king, but the odds are against it and that second king will be visible, thus driving down your possible earnings.

Also drop out on a small pair—someone else will almost invariably get a larger one. Drop out on any non-pair where one card is below ten and the hole card is below king. It is best to have the better card unexposed; it opens up your strategy instead of revealing the best part of your hand to your opponents.

In seven-card stud, the advice is similar, but there are more opportunities for betting. At the first betting interval, you will have been dealt two cards down and one up. Stay in for the fourth card if you have three of a kind, any pair, any pair with an ace or king as the third card (or kicker), or a three-card straight or flush. If you have a low pair, including a pair with an ace or king kicker, drop out after the fourth card if your hand does not improve. On three-card straights or flushes, stay in until the fifth card and drop then if the hand does not improve to a four-card or full strength or flush. Following are a few sample games of seven-card stud. Again you are the fourth of six players. Here is the third round as the deal appears to you:

Seven-card Stud #1

Player 1	?	?	A
Player 2	?	?	J
Player 3	?	?	3
Player 4	7	J	J
Player 5	?	?	8
Player 6	?	?	K

Player one opens the betting; player two stays, as does player three. You have a pair of jacks and stay for one more round. Player five and six also stay.

Generally in seven-card stud most players will stay through the first few rounds no matter what they have. The average player assumes his chances of getting something good are better here than in a five-card game, and if he drops out, he loses all chance of winning. Staying past the second betting interval on poor cards often can prove costly. Players who stay in too long will lose; players who fold if they do not have the cards can win. In the fourth round, the deal now looks like this:

Player 1	?	?	A	8
Player 2	?	?	J	J
Player 3	?	?	3	7
Player 4	7	J	J	Q
Player 5	?	?	8	7
Player 6	?	?	K	Q

Now, what are your expectations? You cannot improve on that pair of jacks since player two has the remaining two jacks. Two sevens and one queen also show, meaning that only one seven and two queens can improve your hand. There are no assurances. Get out.

Seven-card Stud #2

This time we will expose the hole cards for each player and show how staying in can prove costly. Remember that each player is unaware of the others' hole cards. This is the third round of the deal:

Player 1	(3)	(7)	A
Player 2	(A)	(K)	3
Player 3	(Q)	(Q)	7
Player 4	(8)	(8)	8
Player 5	(5)	(6)	4
Player 6	(J)	(10)	J

Player one and two should drop out immediately. A pair, a three-card flush, or straight are essential for staying with the fourth card. Instead, however, player one opens the betting at $2; player two follows suit. Player three, who has a nice pair tucked away, raises $2. Player four, who wants to keep as many people in the betting as possible, just sees the bet. Player five, who is looking for a small straight also meets the current bets, as does player six. Players one and two meet the raise, and there is now $24 in the pot. Round four looks like this:

Player 1	(3)	(7)	A	K
Player 2	(A)	(K)	3	A
Player 3	(Q)	(Q)	7	7
Player 4	(8)	(8)	8	9
Player 5	(5)	(6)	4	Q
Player 6	(J)	(10)	J	10

Everyone is encouraged to stay in, though that queen did nothing for player five and it reduced the chances of player three's making a full house with queens up. Player one should drop but does not. Player three opens the betting at $2. Player four again stays in but does not raise. Player five is on shaky ground but stays for the fifth card. Player six raises $2; player one drops out, but all the others see the raise. The pot is now $46; each player has invested $8, player one putting in $6 before bowing out to the inevitable. The next round looks like this:

Player 1	(3)	(7)	A	K	(folded)
Player 2	(A)	(K)	3	A	J
Player 3	(Q)	(Q)	7	7	10
Player 4	(8)	(8)	8	9	9
Player 5	(5)	(6)	4	Q	7
Player 6	(J)	(10)	J	10	Q

Player four with two nines showing bets first. He bets $5, upping the standard bet to scare some players out—those who might luck into improving over his eights-over-nines full house—and to convince others that the pair of nines made his hand, thus making it appear that he simply has three nines, a seemingly beatable hand for anyone with a higher three of a kind or a possible straight. Player five, encouraged by the fifth card, stays further. Player six has been hurt badly by the round. He needs additional jacks and tens for his full house, and one of each has already been played. He stays, but reluctantly.

Player two stays on his two aces but should drop. It is apparent that player four has at least three of a kind. There is only one ace in the deck or exposed; it is the only card that can help, while there are thirty-three cards not yet exposed or dealt that can hurt. Thus a one in thirty-three chance of winning. The risk outweighs the profits.

Player three also stays, even though his chances for a full house were also limited by the last deal when the final queen and another seven were dealt. Another $25 goes into the pot, bringing it to $71 and each player's investment to $13. The sixth round looks like this:

Player 1	(3)	(7)	A	K	(folded)	—
Player 2	(A)	(K)	3	A	J	J
Player 3	(Q)	(Q)	7	7	10	6
Player 4	(8)	(8)	8	9	9	6
Player 5	(5)	(6)	4	Q	7	9
Player 6	(J)	(10)	J	10	Q	9

Player two has a pair of jacks for high showing and thus opens the betting. He is encouraged by the new pair, but opens low at $2. He still should fold since the odds of hitting a full house are pretty stiff with one ace and one jack already exposed.

Player three has only one chance to improve—hitting the remaining seven for a full house. At a $2 bet, he decides to go ahead. Player four wants to drive out some players and raises $10.

Player five still needs a three or an eight to hit his straight. There is only one card of each denomination showing, thus there are six cards out of a possible twenty-eight unexposed in the deck that can help. The pot is now $87 and the bet $12. The risk is six out of twenty-eight. The probable payoff is higher than the risk, so player five stays in. But he has carried the straight far enough already and should drop out. The hand is becoming too costly.

Player six now has a possible straight if he gets a king or an eight and a possible full house if he gets a ten. One king, two jacks, one ten, and one eight have been exposed, leaving seven cards to help him out of twenty-eight. This leaves him with a good winning probability. Player six raises another $8 on this probability. The pot is $99 when it reaches him, his bet is $20 for a 4-1 payoff on a 7 in 28 or one in four, or a 3-1 risk. Player two has already bet $15; it will now cost him $18 more to stay in. If he is dumb he stays. He has been dumb all along, but he drops, as does player three. Player four and five see the final raise. The last card is dealt face down. Exposed, the final deal looks like this:

Player 1	(3)	(7)	A	K	(folded)	—	—
Player 2	(A)	(K)	3	A	J	J	(folded)
Player 3	(Q)	(Q)	7	7	10	6	(folded)
Player 4	(8)	(8)	8	9	9	6	(3)
Player 5	(5)	(6)	4	Q	7	9	(6)
Player 6	(J)	(10)	J	10	Q	9	(4)

No one has improved on this round. Neither player five nor six has a pair showing. It is unlikely then that either has a full house; most of the cards that could help them in this direction are exposed in other hands. It is likely that each has a straight. Player five can only beat player four if he has a full house with queens on top. Since player six holds one queen, the chances of this are limited. It is also unlikely considering the fact that player five did not raise at all during the game.

Player six could win if he had a ten-high full house, but he is also limited by the exposed cards. Since each has only two cards that can beat him (two unexposed which might combine for a full house), player four decides the odds are with him. He bets $15. Player five folds. Player six is sure according to his betting patterns that player four has at least three of a kind. He cannot beat that at the showdown. He might bluff him out of the pot by substantially raising player four's bet. But he also folds. In this situation it would be worthwhile to bluff if (1) player four seemed nervous and was losing money, (2) player four is easily bluffed, (3) player four is a good player but you feel that you can convince him through an audacious bet that you made that full house. Generally you should not throw good money after bad if you really believe that the other player has the cards to beat you. Do not worry about being bluffed. Only play your cards as far as seems reasonable, then get out.

In this sample game, staying in became costly for several players, even for those players who had reasonable expectations of winning. If player five and player six had continued staying in during the aforementioned situation, they might eventually have profited through the law of averages. Players one through three, however, each played their cards far too long. The chances of winning were too slim and those constant betting intervals started grinding down their money supply. In stud poker, get out as quickly as possible unless you have a winning hand or reasonable chances of drawing one. If you are about to draw the seventh card and you still have not made your hand, do not raise. Get out if you are obviously beaten by at least two other hands.

POKER CHART: ODDS ON MAKING
A HAND IN THE DRAW*

Holding one pair, drawing three cards.
     Two pair, 5—1
     Three of a kind, 8—1
     Full house, 97—1
     Four of a kind, 359—1

Holding one pair, and ace kicker, drawing two cards.
     Aces up, 7½—1
     Another pair, 17—1
     Three of a kind, 12—1
     Full house, 119—1
     Four of a kind, 1080—1

Holding two pair, drawing one card.
     Full house, 11—1

*Providing there are no wild cards or jokers used.

Holding three of a kind, drawing two cards.
Full house, 15½—1
Four of a kind, 22½—1

Holding three of a kind and one other card, drawing one card.
Full house, 14⅔—1
Four of a kind, 46—1

Drawing one card to a four-card straight.
Both ends open. Straight, 5—1
One end open or 4-card inside straight. Straight, 11—1

Drawing one card to a four-card flush.
Five-card flush, 4½—1

Four straight flush, both ends open.
Straight flush, 22½—1

One end open, or inside straight flush, drawing one card.
Straight flush, 46—1

Holding one ace, drawing four cards.
Pair of aces, 3—1
Two pairs, aces up, 14—1

Low Ball and High-Low Poker

Low ball poker is regular poker in reverse. The low hand wins; the ace is counted as the lowest card, two aces are the lowest pair, and straights and flushes do not count in determining low hand. Low ball is played as draw or stud. The lowest hand is A, 2, 3, 4, and 5 and is called a "bicycle." In high-low poker, the pot goes half to the high hand and half to the lowest hand. Straights and flushes count, so A, 2, 3, 4, and 6 is the lowest hand. A player can go for the full pot by having both the best low and best high hand. Since most high-low games are with seven-card hands or wild cards, a player can luck into a high-low hand.

In seven-card, high-low stud, for example, each player can use five cards as high hand and five cards as low hand. Consider this possible hand: A, A, A, 2, 3, 4, and 6. The three aces may win high hand. The other will surely win the low hand.

It is advisable in high-low poker to decide, before the draw or before the betting in stud, which hand you are playing for. Do not purposely go for high-low. Only declare a high-low hand if it falls into your lap. In high-low poker, before the final betting interval (after the draw in the draw version and after the final card is dealt in stud), each player declares whether he is trying for the high pot, the low pot, or both. If you try for high-low and one hand is beaten, but the other is best, you lose everything. Only declare high-low if your cards seem a near certainty to win. Otherwise, take the safe route.

It has been previously explained how to play for a high hand. The following hands show how to play for a low hand in high-low or low ball poker.

Low ball hand #1

This is low ball draw. These are your cards: K, K, 3, 2, and 4. Drop. Do not discard the two kings and draw. Never draw more than one card at low ball. Never keep a card above eight in your hand. Most winning low ball hands will contain no pairs and will also contain no face cards. By discarding two cards, you are geometrically increasing your chances of drawing a pair.

Low ball hand #2

Again the game is draw, your cards are A, 6, 3, 2, and K. Discard the king and draw. You are looking for a card below nine. Drawing just one card means there is less chance of getting a card to destroy your hand. If you do draw a six, three, two, or an ace in this situation, it is unlikely that you will win. Paired hands usually lose. Fold.

Low ball hand #3

This is low ball stud. You are the fourth player and the deal looks like this after the third card is dealt:

Player 1	?	?	K
Player 2	?	?	6
Player 3	?	?	7
Player 4	K	6	3
Player 5	?	?	J
Player 6	?	?	Q

With the low three, you open the betting. So far you are okay, but just bet lightly until you are sure that future cards will not destroy your hand. The next card is dealt:

Player 1	?	?	K	J
Player 2	?	?	6	7
Player 3	?	?	7	3
Player 4	K	6	3	2
Player 5	?	?	J	Q
Player 6	?	?	Q	4

The deuce is low; you bet again but still lightly. Players one and four should drop out—even without knowing what additional cards they hold. Those two face cards mean that each hand depends on hitting three consecutive low cards without getting a pair and without getting a card above eight. The chances are prohibitive. All six players, however, stay in. The next deal looks like this:

Player 1	?	?	K	J	10
Player 2	?	?	6	7	4
Player 3	?	?	7	3	2
Player 4	K	6	3	2	K
Player 5	?	?	J	Q	9
Player 6	?	?	Q	4	4

Player three is now low with 2, 3, and 7 showing. He opens the betting. That pair of kings just about busts your hand. The following cards can hurt you: another king, two queens, two jacks, three tens, three nines, two sixes, two threes and two deuces. That's seventeen cards out of a total thirty-two that are unexposed or still in the deck. There is $30 in the pot and the bet is $5. The chances are approximately even, but the payoff is 5-1. Stay, but only for one more card. Player one drops out; the others stay. The sixth deal looks like this:

Player 1	?	?	K	J	10	(folded)
Player 2	?	?	6	7	4	3
Player 3	?	?	7	3	2	A
Player 4	K	6	3	2	K	A
Player 5	?	?	J	Q	9	10
Player 6	?	?	Q	4	4	3

Players two and three evidently have seven high-low hands. Players five and six seem obviously out of the running. To be assured of winning against both players two and three, you have to draw either a four or a five. A six, three, two, or ace will result in a pair. An eight is higher than their exposed top card; a seven merely equals the top card and may lose to player two if one of his hole cards is lower than your six. There are four fives and one four available in the deck. Five cards can help out of the twenty-seven left unexposed. The bet is $10. The pot has $60 in it. The payoff is 5-1 on a 9-2 risk. It is not much of an edge, but let us assume you took the chance.

On the final deal you receive a ten. It is likely to be a losing hand and you fold. Player three wins as the holder of that final four and this hand: 7, 4, 3, 2, and A. In low-ball seven-card stud poker it is best to drop on the third card or the fourth card if you have drawn two cards higher than eights. If the fifth card drawn gives you two cards above eight, play one more card if the bet is low enough. But pay strict attention to the cards already exposed and your opponents' likely hands. Do not continue buying cards unless there is a good chance of winning. Drop if you are beat by the fifth or sixth card and are still looking to make your hand. In the above example, for instance, player four should have dropped after the sixth card was dealt because the possible winnings did not give him that much of an edge. In general, in low ball draw or stud, do not play out a hand containing a high face card or a low pair. Be very cautious in this variation of poker. Most players are not. You can win by playing only the strongest hands.

Other Major Variations of Poker

Baseball: Seven card stud with all threes and nines wild. If a three is dealt face up, the player holding it must match the pot or drop out. If a four is dealt face up, the player holding it gets another hole card. Avoid this game.

Football: Sixes and fours are wild; a four dealt face up requires the player to match the pot or drop out. A face-up deuce draws another hole card. Avoid this game.

Hold 'em: A popular game among big-time poker players. Each player gets two cards face down. Then five cards are dealt face down in the center of the table. The players start betting, then after this interval, three center cards are overturned. These cards are jointly held by all the players and will be used by each in making his hand. There is another betting interval. Then the final two cards are turned up, one at a time, with betting following each turnover. Only bet at the opening round if you have a face card or a pair as your hole cards. Bet lightly before you see those five cards. You should not bet before the commonly held cards are revealed unless you have good cards because those cards will be used by all the players. It is better to go in with some advantage. The point is to have an edge, not just an equal chance of winning.

Spit in the ocean: Four cards are dealt to each player. The next card in the deck is overturned and used as the fifth card by each player. This card is also a wild card; cards matching it in the players' hands can also be used as wild cards. This is a variation of draw poker, so a draw follows the initial deal. As with all poker variations that feature wild cards, it is best to avoid this game.

Three-card monte: One card is dealt face down and two face up for a three-card hand. Betting follows the deal of each card. A three-card straight flush is the highest hand, followed by three of a kind, simple flush, simple straight, one pair, or high card. Generally stay in for the first face up card, open the betting if your hole card is a face card or an ace. On the second card, stay in only if you have a two-card straight, a two-card flush, a pair, or an ace. Drop on any other hand.

BLACKJACK

The rules of blackjack are fairly simple. The object is to hit or nearly hit a total of twenty-one with two or more cards, without going over that number, or going under the total held by the dealer. Aces count as one or eleven; all face cards count ten; all others count according to their denomination, i.e., eight counts eight, seven counts seven, etc. Hitting twenty-one on the first two cards dealt is called blackjack or a natural. At casinos a natural black-jack pays off at odds of 3-2; in private games the payoff is 2-1. In private games certain combinations such as five cards or more totaling less than twenty-one or three sevens, will sometimes earn bonus payoffs. In casino blackjack, bonus hands are rare although the casinos do allow the options of doubling down, splitting pairs, and in-surance bets. An explanation of these options, plus how to play and win at casino blackjack and how to play private blackjack follows in the next section.

Casino Blackjack

In casino blackjack all players play against the dealer who represents the house. The deal never changes hands. To win, the player has to hit closer to twenty-one than the dealer without going "bust," or over that total. There are usually five to eight players at a standard blackjack game; you do not have to worry about beating the card totals of the other players—all of you are playing individual games against the dealer's hand. In casino blackjack, you make your bet before each hand is dealt. If both you and the dealer hit a natural—blackjack on the first two cards—the bet is a standoff and nobody wins or loses. If the dealer hits a natural and you do not, you lose your bet. If you hit a natural and the dealer does not, he pays you off at 3-2. This part of the game offers a slight edge to the bettor because you do not lose at 3-2 when the dealer hits black-jack, the play comes back to you to decide whether to stand on your hand as dealt or try to get closer to twenty-one. The blackjack dealer is bound by casino rules to draw another card if his two-card total is sixteen or below and bound to stay if his total is seventeen or above. You, however, are not bound by such rules and can draw or stand as you see fit. The standard advice is to stand on anything above sixteen and draw on any hand below twelve. The questionable decisions come on stiffs, or hands of twelve, thirteen, fourteen, fifteen, or sixteen.

In casino blackjack the dealer deals himself one card face up and one card face down. (Depending on the casino your first cards are either all face up, all face down, or one up, one down. It matters little since the casino dealer's actions cannot be affected by your cards. He draws on sixteen or below, stands on seventeen or above.) The dealer's face up card will determine what you do on a stiff hand. If the dealer shows an ace, king, queen, jack, ten, nine, eight, or seven—draw. If the dealer shows a deuce, three, four, five, or six—stand pat. The reasoning is that you can be fairly sure that the dealer has not hit seventeen if he shows a low card, unless his hole card is an ace in which case he has to continue drawinging. The odds are that he will go bust—over twenty-one. If, however, he has a high card showing, your below seventeen hand will likely lose.

This advice is based on the chances over thousands of plays. Often you will draw on thirteen because the dealer showed a queen, then go bust and discover that his hole card was a three. You cannot win them all. But playing this way will increase your percentage of wins. As for staying on seventeen or over, a card total of nineteen or twenty will win most hands; seventeen and eighteen will win or at least tie more than their share since the dealer will often go bust trying to reach these numbers. It is just plain stupid to throw away a probable winning hand by trying to get closer to twenty-one. Never draw over seventeen; there are few cards that can help you and most cards will bust your hand. Failing to draw when your hand is below twelve is also stupid. If you have a ten, for example, drawing another card means you may hit a twenty-one, twenty, nineteen, eighteen, or seventeen total—likely winners. Ten only wins if the dealer goes bust. The other numbers can win either by merit or if the dealer goes bust: two chances to win instead of one.

The estimated casino house advantage in blackjack is about 6 percent. This advantage can be reduced through the preceding advice; it can be further reduced when the player takes advantage of the double down, splitting pairs, and insurance options. Explanations of these options follow.

Doubling down: Depending on the casino, the player is allowed the option of doubling his bet if the total of his first two cards hits nine, ten, or eleven. Some casinos permit all three numbers; others permit only the eleven double down. You are permitted to draw only one additional card on a double down. But consider that you, as a player, have received a two-card total of eleven. The dealer does not have blackjack, otherwise he would have already collected your bet and dealt a new hand since a natural for the dealer is an immediate loser to you. There are sixteen cards in the deck that can give you twenty-one; another four can give you twenty; any of the four eights can give you nineteen; any of the four sevens can give you eighteen. There are quite a few chances to draw to a probable winning hand. Your chances of winning at this moment are greatly increased. Double your bet. Always take advantage of a double down situation. The nature of casino blackjack is such that you bet before seeing your cards. This is the one instance where you can bet knowing your full chances.

Splitting pairs: You have been dealt two eights. A perfectly rotten hand. Sixteen is a likely loser; drawing another card is a likely bust. So you split the pair, drawing new cards to each eight, placing a new bet on the second hand, equal to the size of your initial bet. A split hand is the same as a regular hand and you can draw as many cards as seems necessary. On the first eight, you draw a ten for an eighteen, a much better hand. The second eight draws a three, giving you a chance to double down on the eleven total; you thus double your bet on the second hand. You draw a king for a total of twenty-one, a sure winner.

Some pairs, however, should not be split. Never split fives or tens. Two tens, or twenty is a fine hand; two fives or ten points is a good start toward a twenty or twenty-one hand. Always split aces or eights. Split nines unless the dealer's face up card is a seven, a ten-point card, or an ace. Your eighteen will beat or tie any combination with his seven. It is best not to double your hands if the dealer is holding a strong ace or a low point card; if he has twenty or a similar high total it could mean that you will lose two hands instead of one. Likewise, do not split pairs of deuces, threes, fours, sixes, or sevens when the dealer shows a high card. Such low cards are difficult to build solid hands on; if the dealer seems to be holding good cards, do not double your risk. However, if the dealer is showing a low card, remember that his chances of going bust are greatly increased because of the casino regulations that he has to keep drawing on sixteen or below. Double your hands in this situation and stand pat on twelve or more.

Insurance: The dealer deals himself one card up and one card down, but he is not allowed to look at the down card unless the face-up card is an ace or a ten-point card. If it is one of these, he then checks to see if he has a natural blackjack. Otherwise the dealer does not look at the hole card until every player has completed drawing or standing on his hand. This is to prevent tip-offs on the dealer's hand and cheating by either dealer or player. If the dealer has an ace as his up card, before he checks on whether he has blackjack, he offers insurance to the bettors. An insurance bet wins if the dealer's hole card does, in fact, give him blackjack. This bet pays off at odds of 2-1. The bet loses if any other card is the dealer's hole card; when the bet loses, the dealer does not announce which card it is, he just collects your money. Insurance bets are often recommended as a saver when you have a strong hand that can be beaten or tied by blackjack. However, the only time you should bet insurance is when you have a weak hand and you have noticed that a disproportionate number of ten-point cards still remain in the deck. Otherwise avoid the bet.

But, how will you know whether there are more ten-point cards left in the deck than usual? This brings us to the method used by all professional and successful blackjack players to further bring down the house advantage in blackjack and create a winning edge for the gambler: counting cards.

Blackjack is played with from one to four decks, depending on the casino. But all blackjack dealing has this in common: the deck is not shuffled after every hand; the deck is not shuffled until nearly all the cards have been played. The player can acquire an advantage if he keeps track of the ten-point cards and aces already played. Dr. Edward O. Thorp, a revolutionary figure in the development of scientific blackjack play, discovered that the odds of the game shift in the player's direction whenever the ratio of non-tens to tens goes below 2¼:1. There are sixteen ten-point cards and thirty-six others in a standard fifty-two card deck for an exact 2¼:1 ratio. The more ten-point cards available to form high point totals, the more often the player beats the dealer. The dealer goes bust more often; the player hits twenty or twenty-one more frequently; each hits blackjack at the same rate, but the player gets paid off at better odds. Any system of winning at blackjack combines the standard rules of when to stand and when to draw, when to double down or split, and the practice of card counting. It is not an easy task and takes a great deal of practice. Casinos have instituted multiple decks, fast deals, and quick reshuffles to counter card counting. But it still can be done. There are several counting methods.

The first thing to realize is that you are looking for a high ratio of ten-point cards or high cards in the deck. You can either count ten point cards vs. cards played, or high cards vs. low cards. The latter method is a bit easier. First consider all nines, tens, jacks, queens, kings, and aces as high cards; do not count eights; count all others as low cards. Keep a running tally in your head, high cards first. Such as eight to ten, or nine to eleven, meaning eight high cards played to ten low, so far; nine high to eleven low played so far, etc. The ratio of high to low should be 1:1, so up your bets if the ratio is above that.

Take for example a count of nine to eleven. The difference is two; add two units to your standard bet. If you usually bet $1, bet $3 on the next hand in this instance. The logic behind this system is that you benefit from high cards; according to the immutable law of averages, you can beat the dealer when you have a less random shot at high point totals. Nine to ace are helpful cards; below eight are harmful. Eight neither hurts nor helps.

The other way is to count ten-point cards against non-tens. In this circumstance you also keep a running tally in your mind of tens played to non-tens. Then up the bets when the tens approach one in three or less played. Your tally on a single deck, for instance, is now 5:12; five tens, twelve non-tens. There are disproportionately more tens left in the deck; the odds are increasingly in your favor.

As the deck gets more and more depleted, card counting becomes more and more effective. Often, however, there will be no discernible pattern. Bet lightly until the ten-point cards are plentiful, then up your bets considerably. It is harder to figure out 2-1 probabilities in your head, so the even-odds count may be more attractive to the casual bettor. Either works well; the ten-point count is more exact.

So far this presupposes a single deck. Try, if at all possible, to play blackjack only in a single deck game. If you cannot, the card-counting recommendations hold, but do not start betting on patterns until at least half of the decks have been used.

Private Blackjack

In private games the multiple deck problem is usually missing, the deals are not as fast, and the dealer does not reshuffle if he catches you counting cards. Thus the private game of blackjack is eminently beatable. In private games, the deal rotates. A player who hits blackjack wins the deal; a dealer keeps the deal until someone else gets blackjack. If two players hit blackjack in one hand, the deal passes to the player closest to the dealer's left.

In private games, dealing has a number of advantages not present in casino blackjack. The dealer still plays his hand against each individual player, but the dealer now wins in case of a tie and the players each pay the dealer 2-1 odds if he hits a blackjack. In casino blackjack, bets are canceled on ties and the players pay off at even money to a dealer's natural. The dealer can also draw or stand at will; he can stand on sixteen or less or draw on seventeen if it is necessary to beat a player's hand.

The betting is also slightly different in the private game. In private games the first card is dealt face down, the second card face up. Betting begins after the first card is dealt, each player risking a particular sum on his hand against the dealer's. The dealer has the option, if he has a strong hole card, to double all bets against his hand. The players, then, can drop out before the second card, meet this raise, or redouble it. All players must meet this double to stay in. After the second card is dealt, the dealer pays off at 2-1 on any blackjack unless he also holds a natural. In case of ties, the dealer wins, but only the amount of the player's bet, not at 2-1 odds. The decision then comes back to each player whether to draw or stand pat.

Splitting pairs is allowed in private blackjack, but doubling down and insurance usually are not. The play of a private game after the first two cards are dealt should be governed by the same rules that apply to the casino game. A summary of the rules on when to draw, when to stand, and when to split pairs follows.

1. Always stand on seventeen or above.
2. Always hit on eleven or below.
3. Hit on twelve, thirteen, fourteen, fifteen, or sixteen if the dealer's exposed card is ace, king, queen, jack, ten, nine, eight, or seven.
4. Stand pat if the dealer's exposed card is deuce, three, four, five, or six.
5. Always split aces or eights.
6. Never split fives or tens.
7. Split nines if the dealer's exposed card is deuce, three, four, five, six, eight, or nine.
8. Do not split deuces, threes, fours, sixes, or sevens unless the dealer's exposed card is a seven or less.

Since in private blackjack you are able to see your first card before betting, this provides you with a decision lacking in the casino game: how much to bet and when? If your first card is an ace or ten, bet big. If it is a seven or below, bet small. Say your standard betting unit is $2. Bet $6 on the ace, $4 on the ten; bet $1 on the seven, six, five, four, three, or two. (These are poor building cards.) Bet the standard $2 on an eight or nine. If you are dealing and your first card is an ace, double the player's bets against you. If you have dealt yourself a ten-point card, double only if the other players have bet lightly, thus indicating weak hands. If you, as a regular player, hold an ace as the first card and the dealer doubles, redouble his bet. Never double or redouble on less than an ace or ten-point card.

Raise your bets even further if by your calculations the deck is heavy in high or ten-point cards. Counting cards is somewhat easier in private blackjack; the advice from casino blackjack still applies. Either count high cards vs. low cards or ten-point cards vs. non-tens, then bet higher when the ratio changes in your favor; bet lighter when there are fewer good cards left in the deck to aid your hand.

BACCARAT AND CHEMIN DE FER

Both baccarat and chemin de fer are similar to blackjack but the object is to hit nine or as close to it as possible. Face cards and tens count ten points or zero; others their denominational value. The best hand is a natural nine: the two-card total hits nine. The next best hand is a natural eight. If a player has a seven and a six, the total is not thirteen but three since all tens are disregarded; thus it is impossible to have a bust hand.

Each player plays against the dealer; two cards are initially dealt to the player and to the dealer. If neither player nor dealer has a natural, the player can stand on his hand or draw to hit nine. In most variations, the player

90

against the dealer must draw to four or under or stand pat on six or seven, and he can do either with a total of five. This draw card is face up, the others are face down. If the player draws an ace, face card, or ten, the dealer then must stand on four and above and draws one more card to a two, three, or one. If the player draws a nine, the dealer stands on four and above, draws on two or one, and can do either on his three-count hand. If the player draws an eight, the dealer stands on three and above, draws to two or one. If the player's draw is seven or six, the dealer stands on seven and draws to lower. On a five or four draw, dealer stands on six and above and draws to lower; on a three or two draw, the dealer stands on his five-count hand or above and draws to lower. If the opposing player stands, however, the dealer stands on six or seven and draws to five or under.

In some variations players are given a choice of standing or drawing when they are the deal, but the wisest course is to play this way—it offers the dealer his best chance to win. These are rules for both baccarat and chemin de fer, but baccarat has an added variation. When the dealer is playing a particular player, he deals a third hand and the player can play either hand not held by the dealer. He may also bet a cheval. This is a bet on both hands against the dealer. The player wins only if both hands beat the dealer. The cheval is lost only if both hands lose to the dealer.

In both games the deal rotates. The person who is dealing plays against each player in the game, one at a time, in succession. The dealer announces at the beginning of his deal the size of his bank; the other players then declare what part of his stake they wish to play for. A player can call "banco" and play for the entire stake, which means the other players are shut out until the next deal. In chemin de fer, the deal continues until the dealer loses a decision. In baccarat the dealer continues until he is totally wiped out or relinquishes the deal voluntarily.

Baccarat was the game that acquired millionaire industrialist John W. Gates his colorful nickname (Bet-a-Million). One day, according to an account by Bernard Baruch, Gates set his baccarat bank at $1 million; another bettor went banco on him and tried a cheval. Gates won the first hand but lost the second, canceling the bet and driving the faint-hearted observer Baruch from gambling. It is not suggested that a casual player try Gates' trick. But it is suggested that if the stakes are high, try a cheval—it is a safer bet than risking everything on one hand. It is also recommended that you look for those chemin de fer and baccarat games in which the draw is not regulated. You will always draw to the preceding patterns, but if the draw is not regulated, some players are likely to be careless or incompetent. There is no other way to get an edge in either game. Winning is a matter of luck, though the payoffs—unlike in casino games of chance—are equal to your chances of winning. You are just betting even against the dealer. Both games are available in most casinos.

GIN RUMMY

There are endless variations of rummy from gin rummy to knock rummy to five hundred to Oklahoma, and onward. The basic gambling game is gin rummy, so this chapter will cover that two-man game exclusively: how to play, score, and win. First the basic rules.

A standard fifty-two card deck is used; each player is dealt ten cards. The twenty-first card is dealt face up. This is called the up-card and the non-dealer has the option of picking up this card and using it in his hand or refusing it and selecting the top card from the remaining thirty-one cards in the deck. After taking the up-card or the top deck card, the player must discard one of the cards in his hand. Each hand has to consist of ten cards at all times. The dealer next has the option of taking this face-up discard or the top card in the deck. After selecting a card, he also must discard one card on the face-up discard pile.

The object of the game is to form sets of consecutive cards in one suit, or cards of one denomination. A set is not considered complete until it has three or more cards in it; otherwise a card is considered unmatched and will count against the player at the end of the game. A legitimate sequence would be the three, four, and five of clubs; an unmatched sequence would be the four and five of clubs. Likewise, three jacks would be a complete set; two jacks would not.

If a player fills his hand—gets all cards in completed sequences or sets—he discards his eleventh card face down and announces gin. The opponent's non-matched cards are added and scored against him. All face cards count ten points, aces count one, and all other cards count according to their denomination.

Gin is an immediate winner, but it is also possible to end the game through knocking. If you have ten points or less in your hand, it may be advisable to end the game this way. The knocker also lays his final discard face down and announces that he is knocking. The knocker lays his hand out on the table and his opponent is then given an opportunity to "lay off" his unmatched cards on the knocker's hand. For example, the knocker's hand looks like this: J, 10, and 9 of clubs; 7, 7, 7; 2, 3, and 4 of diamonds, 5 of clubs. The five is the only unmatched card; thus the knocker's total count is five. The opponent's hand looks like this: K, Q, 8, and 7 of clubs; 10, 10, 10; 8, 8, 8. The opponent lays off his clubs against the knocker's clubs, leaving him with no unmatched cards. This is called ginning off, and the opponent thus collects bonus points. Had the opponent been unable to lay off all four unmatched cards, they would have been added up, and the knocker's total would be subtracted from this number. The knocker wins if his total is less than his opponent's total. If the opponent had been able to lay off all but five or less points, the knocker would have lost. This is called underknocking and is also awarded bonus points.

This is the basic game; scoring can get a bit complicated. If a player gins, he gets twenty-five bonus points plus all the points in his opponent's hand. If a player successfully knocks, he gets all the points in his opponent's hand minus the points held in his own hand. If a player underknocks, he gets a bonus of twenty points plus the total points in his opponent's hand. If the opponent gins off on a knock, he gets a bonus of thirty points, plus the points in the knocker's hand. The first player to receive one hundred points gets an additional one hundred points plus twenty points bonus for each winning hand. This player then subtracts his opponent's total score from his own, giving the loser an additional twenty points for each of his winning hands. The subtracted total is the final score. If the opponent has had no winning hands, this is called a "schneider." In the gambling version of gin rummy, players will assign a monetary value to each point; the loser has to pay off according to the number of points acquired by the winner multiplied by the betting unit. In small games, a penny a point is common.

There are other scoring variations, but the aforementioned is the easiest method and thus is recommended. The Hollywood version employs columns, bonus boxes, double scoring on spade upcards, and at least a dozen separate scoring rules. When playing any gambling game, get the rules down to a bare minimum. Complicated scoring mechanisms favor whoever keeps score. The more complex scoring variations are based on the simple method; they do not change the proportions of bonuses offered for knocking, underknocking, or ginning. Thus there is little need for an additional scoring method. It is better to worry about playing strategy than scoring. Scoring variations will not have an effect on the recommended strategy for winning at gin rummy.

Basically, the player has to know two things: which sequences or sets to go for on the initial hands, and when to knock. For example, if you are dealt A, A, A; ten of hearts; ten of spades; seven of clubs; six of clubs; four of diamonds; three of diamonds; and three of clubs, which cards should you get rid of, which cards should you keep? Keep the three aces, of course; keep the threes and the four; keep the six and seven. Work on drawing to these cards instead of the ten. Get rid of any unmatched high point cards if at all possible. There are two cards—ten of clubs and ten of diamonds—that will match those tens. There are two cards—five of clubs and eight of clubs—that will turn the six-seven into a matched sequence. The chances are equal, but if your opponent gins or knocks while you hold the higher cards, you are left holding more points. Also if he knocks, it is usually easier to lay off two cards that are not part of a pair than it is to lay off a pair.

Consider that the tens can only be laid off a matched sequence; the seven and six can be laid off as part of a club sequence, a six set, or a seven set. Play every hand as if it were going to end on the next card. Keep down the point total in your hand at all times. It should be obvious why you keep the 4, 3, 3 sequence. You can be helped here by the five of diamonds, the deuce of diamonds, the three of hearts, and the three of spades. This doubles the improvement chances of the tens or six-seven proposition. Keep low cards; discard high cards. Keep unmatched cards that can be made in more than one way—i.e., a run or three of a kind.

As for knocking, the points awarded this are far below that of gin, underknocking, or ginning off. Be very wary of knocking, particularly if you have a hand full of sequences rather than sets. (A sequence is three or more consecutive cards in a suit; a set is three or four cards of one denomination.) It is much easier to lay off on a sequence than a set. The ideal hand to knock would be something like this: 10, 10, 10, 10; 3, 3, 3, 3; A, A. The aces count two points and there are no threes or tens remaining to lay off.

Knock only if your unmatched point total is five or less and no more than one open-ended sequence in your hand, or if you have achieved this low-point total within the first five cards drawn after the deal. These may be the only instances where you can catch an opponent flat-footed. Otherwise, wait for gin and get rid of those high point cards.

3

Games of Chance

The games covered in this chapter can all be described as games of chance. Winning is totally dependent on luck; skill at the game can rarely affect the outcome. The game is totally out of your control and the house—whoever is running the game—takes such a cut that you do not get paid off at the proper odds. In roulette, for instance, there are thirty-eight numbers, but the payoff for betting any single number is only 35-1. Likewise, in the numbers racket, the payoff is 599-1, or $600 for $1, for selecting the right three digit number for that day. Yet there are one thousand such numbers (000 to 999), so the odds against selecting it are one in a thousand.

In the following games, you have a double handicap: It takes luck to win and you cannot control luck; and the takeout by the house reduces the payoff to less than is justified by the odds or chances of winning a bet. This means, of course, that in the long run you are likely to lose. You may win, but it will be very difficult to maintain any consistency unless you are phenomenally lucky.

The games of chance considered here include roulette, craps, keno, chuck-a-luck, slot machines, fortune wheels, bingo, numbers, and the lottery. All these games are won occasionally, but they cannot be beaten. And anyone who promises to provide a system for making a profit at any of these games (with the possible exceptions of roulette or private craps) is a charlatan. But in each game there is a way to minimize your losses and maximize your winnings. The skill in these games is in knowing how and when to bet. Do not expect to win a fortune or make a living betting these games. But a little knowledge can keep you from financial ruin.

Before discussing the games themselves, let us look at betting systems. Since games of chance are so dependent on luck, there are a number of progression betting systems that will supposedly result in an eventual profit for the gambler. Do not believe it. Particularly watch out for progression, or Martingale, betting, or the cancellation systems. In the Martingale system, the bettor bets one color, or number, or bets against or for the shooter (depending on the game), every time. He starts off with, for example, a $1 bet and then doubles it if he loses. He keeps doubling the bet until he wins.

If he does this in roulette, for example, he may put $1 on red. The payoff odds are even, and the chances are that the color will come up almost half of the time (eighteen of the thirty-eight numbers are red). But there are no assurances that the color will come up even once in any ten or fifteen or more straight bets. By continually doubling the bet, the gambler will be betting $512 per spin by the tenth bet. Many casinos limit a roulette bet to $500, so if he loses this one he is stuck with the $500 loss. If there is no limit, by the fifteenth bet he is now wagering $16,384 on one turn of the wheel. After losing this, the gambler walks out of the casino and throws himself in front of the first available bus.

In the cancellation system, the bettor also increases his bets after a loss. But this can obviously get very expensive. There is never any guarantee in a game of chance that you will win on any bet or series of bets. But with the progression betting systems, there is the guarantee that one losing streak will wipe you out.

In other systems, the bettor decreases the amount of his bet while losing and increases it while winning. This may limit your losses if you are on a losing streak, but it will not necessarily increase your winnings. Luck cannot be controlled. If you increase the amount of your bets while you are on a winning streak, you could greatly increase your winnings. However, even a short losing streak could now wipe you out. But if you "feel lucky," go ahead with this type of system since you will be riding with good luck and tailing off on bad. But always, when you are increasing your bets, play with the casino's money, save your own and keep a little each time you win. Do not throw the whole bankroll on each succeeding bet.

No one is that lucky. You will inevitably lose. Every gambler dreams of parlaying a few dollars into a fortune, but unless you keep some money back, there will come a final reckoning.

Apropos of that, gambler Phil Bieber tells the story of how he and his older brother Isadore one day parlayed $20 into $120,000 at Empire City race track in Yonkers, N.Y. After each race they won, they dumped the whole bankroll on the succeeding selection, until six races later they had $120,000. The following night they dumped the whole bundle on Sharkey in the Dempsey-Sharkey fight. After the third round, as Phil tells it, "it looked like Sharkey was a winner so everyone came to my brother to try to hedge their bets." The other gamblers tried to buy $20,000 to $30,000 worth of Bieber's action on Sharkey, but Izzy refused. "All or nothing," the elder Bieber said. In the next round Dempsey knocked Sharkey out. On the ride home a disgruntled Phil Bieber said to his brother, "I can't fault you for your big bets because if you didn't bet big, we couldn't have run $20 into $120,000, but we're horse people not fight people. Why couldn't you have bet $100,000 and kept $20—$20,000 isn't hay.''

His brother replied, ''Oh, for Christ sakes, Phil, shut up. All we lost was $20.''

Unless you can adopt that attitude, stay away from parlaying your bets.

Nevertheless, the following is a description of each game of chance commonly played in the United States or other casinos, how to play, how to bet, and your chances of winning.

CRAPS

There is a scene in *Guys and Dolls* in which the gangster from Chicago, Big Julie, decides he has lost enough in Nathan Detroit's crap game and will begin using his own dice. His dice are blank—no spots whatsoever—and each time he shoots, he miraculously makes his point. The others in the game cannot see any spots on the dice, but they do not question Big Julie's opinion because, like all gangsters from Chicago, Big Julie packs a rod. Big Julie is shooting against Nathan Detroit, who until the new dice arrive is a big winner. Now his cash supply is dwindling because no one can beat a shooter who makes all his points.

In the long run at casino crap games, every crap bettor is Nathan Detroit; the house is that gangster from Chicago; and the dice may as well be blank for all the chance you have of winning.

In casino crap games the odds are always against you. There is no way that you can ever get the odds to favor you. You can reduce the percentage against, but there will never come a time when you can manipulate the betting so that you are sure to win. The casino never pays off at the correct odds on a proposition; often the odds offered are ridiculously low and the house advantage far higher than the standard 1.4 percent.

In private crap games you have a better chance of winning, if no one is running the game and taking a cut. In fact, in private crap games if you bet against the shooter, you will win in the long run. However, this is only in private games, and the greatest access to dice games is in the public, legal and illegal, casinos, and those games are unbeatable. The casino variety, called bank craps, is a game of sheer chance. If you are lucky, you will win. If you are unlucky, you will lose. If you are stupid, you will lose a lot more. The game is out of your control and in the long run—if you keep playing long enough—you will be a lifetime loser.

That said, you can maximize your winnings on the days luck is running with you. No one can promise a system to beat bank craps—it is mathematically impossible—but your chances improve with some knowledge of the game.

Let us begin with some rules and definitions. The player who throws the dice is called the "shooter." The dice are passed clockwise around the dice game layout. The number thrown is derived by adding the total number of spots on the top side of both dice after they have stopped rolling. The shooter's first roll is a "come-out". If on the come-out the shooter throws a seven or an eleven, he wins, which is called a "pass." If he throws a crap, two, three, or twelve, he loses. If he throws any other number, it becomes his "point." He then continues throwing until he hits that particular number again, or he throws a seven. He wins by hitting the point before hitting seven. Seven is a losing number except on the come-out. If the shooter throws a seven, which is called a "miss-out," he then relinquishes the dice to the player on his left. The shooter, by the way, can pass the dice anytime before the miss-out if he wants to.

Those are the basic rules. At most casinos it is necessary for the shooter to bank the dice against the backboard of the dice table layout. Otherwise, the roll does not count. And in all games, players can decline to shoot and can leave the table at any time.

The rules are simple. The actual betting is a little more complicated. Using the standard Las Vegas crap layout, there are several bets offered to the gambler, all at odds less than the chances of winning.

First off, you can bet with or against the shooter on the pass — don't-pass lines. Pass is with the shooter and the player wins if the shooter hits seven or eleven on the come-out or if he makes his point before rolling a seven. The player loses if the shooter rolls a two, three or twelve, called craps, on the come-out or if the shooter hits seven before making his point. Betting with the shooter is called betting "right." Betting "wrong" is betting against the shooter on the don't-pass line. The "wrong" bettor wins if the shooter craps on the come-out or if the shooter hits a seven before making his point. If the shooter hits seven on the come-out or makes his point, the don't-pass bettor loses. The odds would be slightly in favor of the wrong bettor because mathematically the shooter will lose about 1.4 percent more often than he wins. But casinos ban collection on the don't-pass line if either a two or a twelve is rolled on the initial throw. (Some casinos bar two, others twelve.) This means that although the shooter has crapped out, the casino refuses to pay off on that particular number. This knocks down the don't-pass bettors' odds on winning from about 1.4 percent for to about 1.4 percent against.

The odds against the pass bettor in any crap game are 1.4 percent against. Yet the casino pays even odds. That percentage may seem small, but the casino gets it every time the dice roll, and the dice move fast in a crap game, which is why craps is the most popular casino game both with gamblers and casino operators. For the gambler, there is all the action you could possibly want. For the casinos, the suckers' money never stops pouring in.

Come or Don't Come Bets

The bettor can also make come or don't-come bets. Briefly, this is paid off at the same even odds as the pass — don't-pass bet, and the chances of hitting it are the same. Come and don't-come bets are side bets wagered after the shooter has acquired a point. For example, if the shooter hits six on the come-out, this is his point, and now come and don't-come bets will begin. The next roll is considered a come-out for a come bet, meaning that a player who bets come wins on this roll if the shooter hits seven or eleven; he loses if the shooter hits, two, three, or twelve. Any other number becomes the come point, and in order to win the shooter has to hit this number before hitting seven.

The don't-come bettor wins if on the first roll after his wager has been placed, the shooter hits two, three, or twelve. If the shooter hits seven or eleven, the don't-come bet loses. The don't-come bet also wins if after the shooter has acquired a come point, he hits seven before making the point. The come and don't-come bet can only be made after the first come-out, after the shooter has a point to make. Consider this sample of a series of rolls. The shooter hits a six on the come-out. This is his point; he must roll it again before hitting seven in order to win.

Come — don't-come betting is now allowed. The next number rolled is four. This is now considered the come — don't-come point; it is not related to the shooter's point. The next roll is six, the shooter has hit his point and pass bettors win on this shot, but it does not affect the come — don't-come bet. The only numbers to affect the come — don't-come bets in this series are four and seven. The next roll is four; the come bet wins and this number is now the shooter's next point. A come — don't-come bet can only be made when the shooter has a point to be made; although the bet will carry over through a series of rolls until the come-point or seven is rolled.

There are numerous other side bets, including the field bet in which the gambler bets that the next number rolled will be two, three, four, nine, ten, eleven, or twelve. The field numbers pay off at even odds, except for the two and twelve which are generally paid off at 2-1. Still, the field bet is a losing proposition because there are sixteen ways to hit the field number, and twenty combinations of numbers to hit five, six, seven, and eight.

Another side bet is "any crap" in which the player bets that either two, three, or twelve will come up on the next roll. This pays off at 7-1 on an 8-1 proposition. You can also bet a particular number to come up the "hardway." If you are betting four the hardway, for example, this means you will win if four comes up in a combination of 2-2 before seven comes up and before any other four comes up. The odds on hitting four or ten the hardway are 8-1; the casino pays off at 7-1. The odds on hitting six or eight the hard way are 10-1, but the house pays only 9-1. Other bets on a particular roll include proposition and any seven bets. The player can bet that on the next roll the shooter will hit two, three, eleven, or twelve. The odds on hitting a two or a twelve are 35-1; casinos pay 30-1. The odds on hitting a three or eleven are 17-1; the casino pays 15-1. Or you can bet that any seven will come up on the next roll. The odds are 5-1, the payoff 4-1. Finally, you can bet that a six or an eight will be thrown before a seven. These bets are called the "Big 6 and Big 8" on the crap table layout and pay even money for a 6-5 against bet—five chances to hit six or eight, six chances to hit seven.

A favorite with big gamblers is the place bet. It shows numbers four, five, six, eight, nine, and ten. These are the point numbers. Remember two, three, eleven, and twelve cannot be point numbers because they are immediate winners or losers on the come-out. The odds against hitting four or ten are 2-1; hitting five or nine are 3-2 against and six or eight are 6-5. These are the odds on hitting that number before hitting a seven. The casino odds are, respectively, 9-5, 7-5 and 7-6.

An explanation of the odds seems in order here. While the dice can come up any one of eleven numbers (two through twelve), the odds on hitting certain numbers are greater than others. For example, there is only one way to make twelve—two sixes. But there are six ways of making seven: one and six, six and one, two and five, five and two, three and four, and four and three. The number of combinations required to make each number can be expressed in the following chart:

Total of numbers shown on both dice	Possible combinations	Number of combinations
2	1-1	1
3	1-2, 2-1	2
4	1-3, 3-1, 2-2	3
5	1-4, 4-1, 2-3, 3-2	4

Total of numbers shown on both dice	Possible combinations	Number of combinations
6	1-5, 5-1, 3-3, 4-2, 2-4	5
7	1-6, 6-1, 2-5, 5-2, 3-4, 4-3	6
8	2-6, 6-2, 3-5, 5-3, 4-4	5
9	3-6, 6-3, 4-5, 5-4	4
10	4-6, 6-4, 5-5	3
11	5-6, 6-5	2
12	6-6	1

There are thirty-six possible combinations of numbers. The odds in making number twelve, then, are one in thirty-six. The odds on making seven are six in thirty-six or one in six. But the payoffs come nowhere near the chances of making a point. Take the "any seven" bet, for example. While the real odds on hitting a seven on any particular roll are one in six, the casino odds are five for one for a mammoth house advantage of 16.67 percent. The casino advantages in other bets are as follows: 11.1 percent on any crap next roll; 11.1 percent on four or ten the hardway; 9 percent on six or eight the hardway; 9 percent on Big 6 or Big 8; 13.89 percent on next roll field bets; 6.67 percent on the four and ten place bets; 4 percent on the five and nine place bets; 1.51 percent on the six and eight place bets; 1.40 percent on don't pass, and 1.41 percent on pass, come, and don't come.

With these big edges, why would anyone bet on such propositions as hardway or field bets? The reason is primarily action, and it is obvious that the suckers do not know the odds on any proposition. Amateur bettors get sucked in by attractive bets like the field, without really knowing what they are getting into. The field bet looks promising—you get seven numbers at even odds. All you have to beat is five other numbers so it looks like a 7-5 proposition. But, add up the combinations in the field numbers vs. the numbers you do not bet on. The numbers 2, 3, 4, 9, 10, 11, and 12 make only these sixteen combinations: one and one, one and two, two and one, one and three, three and one, two and two, three and six, six and three, four and five, five and four, four and six, six and four, five and five, six and five, five and six, and six and six. Some places double your payoff on two and twelve so this diminishes the house edge slightly. But there are still twenty ways to lose and sixteen ways to win. It is a losing bet.

Is there a way to beat bank craps? Flatly no, but you can come closer if you avoid all those sucker bets and stick with the pass—don't pass, come—don't come and six and eight place bets. These are the only bets that have a reasonable house advantage. You can cut that advantage even further if you learn how to "take and give odds." This is the only bet in which there is no house advantage. However, the hitch here is that in order to make the bet, you have to have a previous bet down on the pass—don't-pass line or on the come—don't-come bar.

Also, since this bet does not favor the house, it is not broadcast in big letters on the crap table layout and the casino dealers do not publicize it. The way to bet the odds follows:

Supposing you have bet with the shooter on the come-out. He hits a ten and as you know the odds on making that point before hitting seven are 2-1 against. You have $20 on the pass line; that bet stays the same, but now you can call for odds and bet $20 at 2-1 that the shooter passes. Since these are the correct odds, the house has no advantage. It still has that advantage on your original bet, but the new bet cuts the total advantage in half to about .85 percent against the bettor. Las Vegas casinos limit the size of your odds bet to that of the original bet, but some gambling houses (in Tahoe or Reno for instance) will allow you to double your odds bet—to $40 in the above situation. This brings the percentage down to .61 percent against. It is really crazy not to take this bet. It reduces the house advantage to near zero and with a bit of luck you could win on any given day. You can also, by the way, give odds as well as take them, betting that the shooter will not make it at the correct odds. In the case cited above, if the shooter hits ten, the bettor gets $40 on the pass bet and $60 on the odds bet, for a profit of $60 on $40 invested. What happens, however, if the bettor is a wrong bettor—against the shooter—what are his odds? They are even better because the wrong bettor, in giving odds, reduces the casino percentage to .83 percent; at casinos permitting double odds, the percentage goes to .59 percent. Again, these are the only sensible bets in bank craps. They will limit your losses on any long series of bets and if you are on a winning streak, taking the odds, by coming close to eliminating the house advantage, can maximize your winnings.

There are other betting systems to consider in bank craps. Some have proved successful, others disastrous. In any of these systems, it is a good idea if you are losing steadily, just to quit. Do not continue on a bad streak; you will start pressing and making stupid mistakes.

The "crossfire" system or partner system: This is based on the idea that dice run in cycles. Sometimes they are hot, sometimes cold. If you can observe a game for awhile without losing too much money, you can catch the pattern and win. (At least that is what proponents of this system claim.) You need a partner for this system. One of you bets right or with the shooter; the other bets wrong. You bet only on the pass—don't-pass line and accept the 1.4 percent bite into your bankroll. At the end of a number of plays, it is likely that one of you will have lost money and the other will have won.

Let us say there were one hundred plays. You have bet on the pass line and are up $75; your partner has bet on the don't-pass line and he is down $77. The dice are hot. Your partner folds, gives you the rest of the bankroll, and you play right until the dice go cold.

There is really nothing wrong with this system and it can keep your losses to a bare minimum—that 1.4 percent house advantage. If the dice are truly hot, you may begin winning for awhile. But the point to consider is that dice are inanimate objects; there is no particular reason for them to go hot or cold—unless they are loaded or the shooter is a mechanic.

This system is recommended to casual gamblers who just want a little fun at small cost. You will not lose much on the initial test run with your partner. You will get plenty of action, and you may even win. But if the dice start running against you, get out as soon as possible. Set a limit on what you are willing to lose, then leave when you reach that. There is nothing more pathetic than a system bettor losing on play after play waiting for the dice to get hot again.

Bet against the high roller: This is a system to be used primarily at games you suspect of being rigged. Eventually, a crooked house will start rigging the game against the gambler with the biggest stack of money. The house does not care about you if it can get your money. Watch how the winning bettor bets, then bet against him. This system was developed by Bernard Baruch, the international financier, who was quite a gambler in his youth. In his autobiography, he reported great success using this system.

Progression betting systems: It is unlikely for a shooter to make six or seven passes in a row. So the progression system of betting suggests starting off betting small against the shooter—say $1. Then double it if you lose. It is true that six, seven, or even ten passes in a row are unlikely. But they do occur and you have no guarantee that they will not occur while you are using the progression system. And, as explained in the introduction to this chapter, because most casinos limit bets to $500, you can only double to the tenth bet anyway.

Even if you do win on that sixth or seventh roll, what do you get? Here's the calculation for a sample progression bet.

> 1st bet: $1, 2nd bet: $2. (now −$3), 3rd bet: $4 (now −$7), 4th bet: $8 (now −$15), 5th bet: $16 (now −$31), 6th bet: $32 (now −$63), 7th bet: $64 (now −$127). On the seventh bet you finally win; your $64 bet at even odds lays off $128, but it has cost you $127 to get there—some profit!

Progression betting is based on a misunderstanding of the law of averages. Over thousands of throws, the number of passes to misses will average out nearly even. But this cannot be projected to mean that in the short run the same ratio of passes to misses will occur. The law of averages really only applies to long series and is often referred to by mathematicians as the law of large numbers.

Instead of upping your bets when you are losing, lower them or quit altogether. Raise your bets only when you are winning and then only by a small percentage; otherwise a short losing streak can bring you back to zero. With proper money management you can cut your losses at bank craps and hold on to your winnings on a hot streak.

While bank craps is a loser's game, you can win at private craps. The game is played the same way, except that there is no house cut and the players bet against each other. Plus, the don't-pass bettor collects on every craps (unlike casinos that do not pay off on either two or twelve, depending on the particular casino).

Private amateur games often use the same layout as the casino game, showing the same bets at the same odds. This is insane because it offers the wrong bettor the same certainty of winning that the casino has. If a right bettor wagers on the field, for example, at even money he is cheating himself because it is a less than even money proposition. To keep from being hustled, memorize the correct odds on hitting any of the common crap bets, then get out of any game that offers you less. (Or if you are a bit dishonest, just bet wrong all the way and you are a sure winner.)

Any point:	2	35 to 1
	3	17 to 1
	4	11 to 1
	5	8 to 1
	6	6.2 to 1
	7	5 to 1
	8	6.2 to 1
	9	8 to 1
	10	11 to 1
	11	17 to 1
	12	35 to 1
Any crap: 2, 3, 12		8 to 1
Field: 2, 3, 4, 9, 10, 11, 12		5 to 4
Six or Eight		6 to 5
Pass or don't-pass		almost even
Come or don't-come		almost even
The hardway		
4 or 10		8 to 1
6 or 8		10 to 1

In an honest game, as well, the correct way to bet is wrong. Dice may seem like a 50-50 proposition, but it can be mathematically proven that the shooter is working against a 1.41 percent disadvantage. This is why in casino craps the house applies no odds-cutting gimmick on the pass line. The house can grind along very well with that pure, predictable cut. How this occurs can be explained.

Let us consider 3,960 rolls on the come-out. There are six ways out of thirty-six of rolling a seven, so you will hit it 660 times; there are two ways of rolling eleven, so it will hit 220 times; and craps will be rolled 440 times. If you hit one of the other numbers, your odds stay the same for hitting your point before hitting seven: there are three ways of hitting four or ten, for instance, and still six ways of hitting seven. So seven will come up first two-thirds of the time if your point is four or ten; four or ten will win only one-fifth of the time. Thus, in 3,960 rolls, you will throw a four 330 times and win 110 times. This is regardless of any rolls that you might throw between the come-out and hitting seven or your point. We are only talking about pass – don't-pass bets. The odds are always 3-36 to win and 6-36 to lose on point four.

How this works out to the shooter's disadvantage is shown on the chart in Appendix B. On the come-out the shooter can lose four ways and can win eight ways. But if no decision is gained on the first roll, he has to move on to make a point and the odds are considerably different. They will never be in the shooter's favor and can be substantially against. At private craps, if you always bet against the shooter, you will even finally eke out a profit. The margin may not be substantial—unless the game is rigged against those betting against the shooter—but it is inevitable. This is the only situation in craps in which the longer you play, the more likely are your chances of winning.

A few words of advice, however. When it comes your turn to shoot, pass the dice; you do not want to bet against your own hand, but it is stupid to bet against a mathematical certainty. Second, always bet an equal amount on the don't-pass line. Leave everything up to mathematics. If you keep changing the amount of your bets, there is no longer a certainty of making a profit. With a little bad luck, you will lose the big bets and win the small ones. Only up your bets during the beginning of a series of play, and keep the amount stationary. In addition, never take into a game more than you can afford to lose. Decide the amount of your bet based on the number of plays required to make this system mathematically sound. The chart here, for instance, is based on 3,690 rolls. You could get by with far less than that. But again, the longer you play, the more inevitable the outcome. Even on a small number of plays, you are unlikely to lose much as long as you keep the bet at the same level, never raising or lowering it.

In private crap games, always watch out for cheating. Craps is not easy to win in an honest game; it is impossible if the game is dishonest. Make sure whoever is throwing the dice hits them against the backboard of the layout or, if there is no backboard, that the dice turn over rather than slide. A dice mechanic can manipulate the number coming up if he can keep the dice from turning. If the game is at casino odds, you have an ethical decision to make. You can make a killing by betting wrong all night (you stand to win at a percentage equal to the casino cut on each bet), or you can inform the other players that the odds are incorrect and tell them the proper odds. It is up to you. If the casino odds are set on the dice layout, chances are the suckers will ignore you and the odds will stay as is.

There is another type of crap game primarily played in the smaller illegal joints across the United States. It is

113

The Las Vegas Double Side dealer Bank Craps layout. The center portion
shows the letters C-E. They stand for Crap and Eleven.

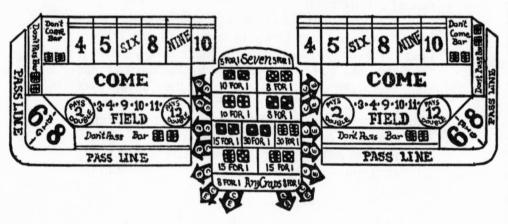

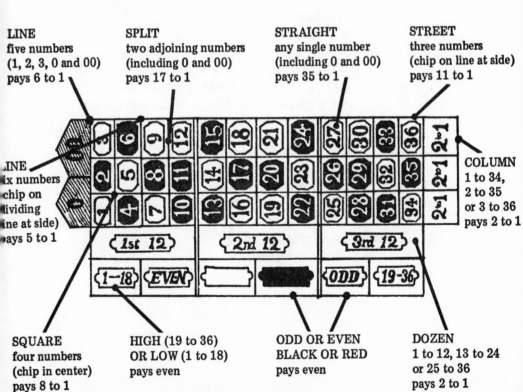

LINE
five numbers
(1, 2, 3, 0 and 00)
pays 6 to 1

SPLIT
two adjoining numbers
(including 0 and 00)
pays 17 to 1

STRAIGHT
any single number
(including 0 and 00)
pays 35 to 1

STREET
three numbers
(chip on line at side)
pays 11 to 1

LINE
six numbers
(chip on
dividing
line at side)
pays 5 to 1

COLUMN
1 to 34,
2 to 35
or 3 to 36
pays 2 to 1

SQUARE
four numbers
(chip in center)
pays 8 to 1

HIGH (19 to 36)
OR LOW (1 to 18)
pays even

ODD OR EVEN
BLACK OR RED
pays even

DOZEN
1 to 12, 13 to 24
or 25 to 36
pays 2 to 1

called open craps and the only difference is that it is played with cash and the house takes a 5 percent cut on each bet booked with it. The players can also bet against each other so that in some bets the odds will approach their proper percentages. But it must again be stressed that in an honest crap game in only one circumstance— betting against the shooter at a private game—can a gambler ever get an edge. There is no way that the gambler can affect the outcome of his bet.

Craps is an extremely popular gambling game because it allows a great deal of personal involvement— everybody gets a chance to shoot the dice, lots of action, several varieties of bets. But the involvement is only an illusion. You can throw the dice, you can throw your money around, but you can never, ever control whether you win or lose.

To sum up, strict attention to the following rules can limit your losses and in certain circumstances can make you a winner. In casino crap games:

1. Only bet pass—don't-pass, come—don't come, six or eight place bets.
2. Bet the odds whenever possible.
3. Do not bet any craps; any seven; the field; big six or big eight; any hardway bet; any single number on the next roll; four, five, nine and ten place bets.
4. Set a ceiling on what you can afford to lose on any one night's play. Leave when you have reached that limit.
5. Avoid all progression betting schemes.
6. Raise your bets only if you are winning.
7. Work with a partner if at all possible.
8. Stay calm; leave when the fast action is causing you to bet too quickly on bad propositions.
9. If you sense a crooked game, get out or bet against the high roller in the game.

In private craps:
1. Always bet against the shooter.
2. Set a limit on what you can afford to lose; quit when you hit the limit.
3. Never accept a bet or a game at casino odds.
4. Pass the dice whenever possible.

ROULETTE

Roulette can be beaten, but it is not easy. The odds are against you. But it can be and has been done—at Monte Carlo, Nevada, South America—any place the numbered wheel has been established as a casino game. Roulette, in fact, is the only casino game based on chance that is beatable. The roulette wheel is a mechanical device with a wood base and metal slots dividing the painted numbers. Normal wear and tear and warpage can cause flaws in the wheel. Certain numbers, series of numbers, or colors can hit more often because of these flaws. And the roulette player who catches these flaws can beat roulette.

The hitch, however, is that the flaws have to be prominent enough to wipe out the stiff house advantage and give the player an edge. But if the flaws are too obvious, the house will get wise and change the wheel. Finding clandestine flaws is not easy, but you can learn how. First, however, an explanation of the game of roulette, the possible bets, and the average player's chances of beating it, is in order.

There are thirty-eight numbers on the standard American roulette wheel: *1—35, 0* and *00*. These numbers are arranged in red, black, and green on the inverted wheel with metal slots, or frets, separating each numbered groove. The wheel is spun around a spindle within its base; the croupier (operator) then throws a small white ivory or plastic ball into the spinning wheel. A number wins if the

115

ball is resting in that groove when the wheel stops spinning. The house pays off the winning number at 35-1 or $36 for every $1 bet. Each number however has a one in thirty-eight chance of hitting, so this diminished payoff gives the house a 2-38 or 5.26 percent advantage. In addition, *0* and *00* are house numbers; a bettor can play either or both numbers, but the house wins all other bets when these numbers come up. Again, this gives the house a two in thirty-eight or 5.26 percent advantage.

This house advantage, and the chances any number has of hitting, are based on thousands of spins. Do not expect any particular number to come up once in the next thirty-eight spins or even the next one hundred. The probability is that a number will hit one hundred times out of 3,800 and the house counts on this overall probability to grind out its profit. Within that range of probability, however, a bettor can win or lose large sums of money because a number hits less or more often than likely. The house will also set a limit on bets so that if it wins against the small bettors and loses against the big bettors, the bank will not be "broken."

In most European and South American casinos (and a few American), the gambler is given a better break. These wheels have only thirty-seven numbers, *1–36*, plus the house number *0*. The chances of hitting a particular number are improved slightly to one in thirty-seven, or 36-1, but the payoffs remain the same—35-1. Thus, the house advantage is cut to one in thirty-seven or 2.75 percent. This is further reduced by the Monte Carlo "in prison" variation. If the ball hits *0* or *00*, a wager on an even odds bet (red or black, high or low, even or odd are even bets) is considered "in prison" and will be returned if the bet comes up on the next spin; a second losing spin and you lose. This cuts the house edge to 1.4 percent, but only for even bets.

116

There have been some predictions that the Nevada casinos will soon begin using the single-zero wheel to attract more customers.

Roulette is not nearly as popular a game in the United States casinos as it is in casinos in the rest of the world. That stiff house takeout is one major reason. Some American casinos have already adopted the single-zero wheel. So the smart gambler would be wise to scout around for a single-zero wheel before playing roulette. Avoid the double-zero wheel if possible and do not go near the triple-zero wheel in some American gyp joints.

The Bets

There are ten variations of bets in standard roulette. The bets and their payoffs are as follows: single number, 35-1; two numbers, 17-1; three numbers, 11-1; four numbers, 8-1; six numbers, 5-1; columns, 2-1; groups, 2-1; red or black, even; even or odd, even; high or low, even. In the single number bet the bettor wagers that the roulette ball will rest on that particular number on the next spin of the wheel. In the two-, three-, four-, and six-number bets the wager is that one of the numbers covered will hit on the next spin.

The roulette wheel contains thirty-six numbers plus the *0* and often the *00*. Eighteen of the numbers on the wheel are red, eighteen are black, and the zeros are green. Players place their bets on a roulette table layout next to the wheel. This layout has all the numbers laid out in three columns with numbers corresponding to their colors on the wheel. (See illustration of roulette layout.) The house numbers are not included in the columns. The first column is topped by the number *1* and contains these numbers: *1, 4, 7, 10, 13, 16, 19, 22, 25, 28, 31* and *34*. The second column is topped by the number *2* and contains these numbers: *2, 5, 8, 11, 14, 17, 20, 23, 26, 29, 32,* and *35.* The third column is topped by the number *3* and contains the numbers: *3, 6, 9, 12, 13, 18, 21, 24, 27, 30, 33,* and *36.* If you bet a column, you get all twelve numbers contained in that column at 2-1 odds, or $3 for every $1 bet. The *0* and *00* are not included in the column, thus the house retains its advantage, paying off at 2-1 odds on a twelve in thirty-eight chance of winning.

The same chances prevail in the group bet. In this bet the player bets a group of twelve numbers: *1—12, 13—24,* or *25—36.* The high-low bet is similar to this, but the player takes eighteen numbers, either *1—18* or *19—36.* The payoff is even or $2 returned for $1 wagered.

Other even odds bets are red or black, and even or odd. In even or odd the bettor wagers that either an even number (numbers divisible by two) or an odd number will occur on the next spin. Zero and double zero are losing spins since they are not considered even or odd.

There are eighteen black numbers and eighteen red numbers; the players can bet a number of one color will come up in the next spin. Green *0* or *00* and the opposite color bet are losers. This bet is the more popular among system bettors, who feel that if a wheel is unbalanced it is more likely to favor one color over another, than a group or column or series of numbers. Also, since the chance on the bet approaches even, the bettor does not have to worry about a long series of defeats before finally winning. Thus the initial investment is lessened.

All the above bets have that same 2-3 or 1-37 house advantage. And even the smartest roulette bettor would be eventually ground down by this percentage were it not for one salient factor: The roulette wheel is a mechanical device and mechanical devices can have flaws. The flaws may not appear until the wheel has been long in use; other wheels may have warps at the beginning. The problem is to find the flaws—or at least the effects of the flaws—before the managers of the casino decide to change the wheel.

If it is a minor flaw and you are not a high roller, the casino may not mind if you start hitting on a flawed wheel. The casino relies on the casual, stupid bettor who is not willing to watch patterns on the wheel before betting. Also roulette wheels are not a small investment and casinos are not always willing to throw out a wheel just because one player has discovered a fault in it. The unbalanced wheel—as well as the bettor who has discovered it—is removed from the casino when the casino operator begins to fear substantial losses.

There are several reasons why a roulette wheel could be flawed: chipped red or black paint on certain numbers, uneven wearing down of the metal slots between the numbers, warpage or cracks in the wooden underside of the wheel, a rotational imbalance, and the general wear and tear of the wheel from being spun and the metal ball being knocked around. If the ball is particularly heavy or the croupier spins the ball on the wheel too fast, damage to the wheel or its grooves can be greatly increased.

Specifically, warpage could cause the ball to favor a certain side of the wheel—a certain series of numbers. Chipped paint on a number can cause the ball to bounce out faster because the groove now lacks some of the porous quality that the paint gives it. As for variations in the metal slots between numbers, even a slightly taller slot may stop the ball from going further. Likewise, a slightly smaller one will never catch the ball and is a sure losing number. If you can crouch down a bit when you first get to the wheel, see if all the slots are parallel or if the wheel is tilted in any way. You may have found a wheel ripe for clocking.

How to Clock

The best way to record the performance of a wheel is with a partner. Too long a stay watching that little ball going around and around could make you dizzy. For the casual bettor who does not have enough time to devote two or three days just for clocking before starting serious betting, only record colors. The house advantage is the same on both bets. Numbers provide bigger payoffs, but the initial investment will be smaller and the final profit, in the long run, will be very similar—if you find an unbalanced wheel. Record the number of plays and the number of times the ball hits red, green or black. A sample work sheet might look like this.

Spins	Red	Black	Green
ЖЖЖ	ЖЖ	ЖЖЖ	Ж
ЖЖЖ	ЖЖ	ЖЖЖ	
ЖЖЖ	Ж		
ЖЖЖ			

Sixty plays, of course, are not nearly enough to discern any pattern. Record for at least four to six hours. If the wheel is balanced, red will appear eighteen times, black eighteen times, and green twice, for every thirty-eight spins. If your final tally is something like this: black 1,260, red 1,260, green 140, give up—you have found a balanced wheel. The only wheel that will qualify for a bet is one that gives a decided edge to one color—an edge substantial enough to win at even odds.

In the example just cited, you recorded 2,660 spins. Suppose black had instead hit only 1,100 times, red 1,400, and green 160. Red is now coming up far more often than eighteen in thirty-eight times—its likely average—and it is beating the eighteen in thirty-eight payoff price. If the pattern holds you can make money off this wheel. Just keep betting red. You will win twenty out of every thirty-eight spins at even money for a substantial profit. Accept for play any color pattern which gives you better than even edge with at least one play per thirty-eight spins. If you intend to spend weeks at the wheel, this could be lowered; it will just take a bit longer to grind out a profit. Do not accept for play a pattern that makes the odds of hitting a color equal to the payoff odds. You can only hope to break even here. If red hits nineteen out of thirty-eight times, the color is beating the house advantage, but it will not mean a profit for you. Move on to another wheel.

It should seem clear that playing a single-zero wheel is a great advantage to a roulette player. To insure a reasonable profit, it is necessary to wipe out the house advantage and create a player edge. On a double-zero wheel, this would require a bias over logical probability of almost 8 percent in favor of your color. This eliminates the 5.26 percent house edge and gives you a one in thirty-eight or 2.63 percent edge. This severe a bias might become obvious too quickly. But the bias on a single-zero wheel can be far subtler. With the in prison variation, you can win with a wheel bias of less than 3 percent; with a single-zero wheel but no in prison variation, you can win with a bias of less than 5 percent.

It may require clocking several wheels before you find one with the necessary bias. This is part of the reason clocking for color is less time consuming than recording the number of times each of thirty-eight numbers occurs over hundreds or thousands of plays. Yet all this time that you are sitting around the roulette table, you will be expected to bet. Until you have found a bias and are ready for serious play, play the minimum amount allowed on one color and stick to that color all through your test run. This will minimize your loses in this stage, while keeping the casino operators off your back. Some casinos set minimums as low as 10 cents, so this betting is unlikely to cost you much. Under no circumstances during the test run should you bet on numbers or columns or groups. The whole idea in recording the spin of the wheel is to eliminate the guess work. There is no reason to lose part of your betting stake before the serious gambling begins.

When you have found a wheel that will assure you a steady profit, split your stake into 250 or more betting amounts. Then bet one unit on each spin of the wheel. Do not increase or decrease the size of your bet until you have hit that number of betting units. The reason for this is that you are playing percentages, not predicting the future.

If the wheel is unbalanced, it will hit your color more often than the other colors. But there is no way of telling in advance on which particular spin your color will hit. If you keep changing the size of your bet, you are leaving part of the decision up to luck—you may win the small bets and lose the big ones. Playing the percentages means waiting as you grind out a profit over hundreds of plays.

Keeping your bet at an even amount will be particularly hard during a run of one color. If your color is red and the wheel has hit five straight black numbers, the temptation is to bet bigger on the next turn. The obvious assumption is that black is hitting more than its probability and such a series cannot be sustained—the law of averages is on red's side. But the law of averages does not and cannot dictate what the next spin will turn up; the chances of red or black coming up are not connected to what has happened in the previous five spins. Overall, if your calculations were correct, red will come up more often than black. On the next spin anything can happen. Also remember that while it may still seem unlikely that black will come up again, you can also get beaten by green, if the house number or numbers come up. Do not play any progression betting schemes; you could get wiped out in a few plays. At the end of your allotted number of betting units, if you are showing a profit, then up the amount of your bets.

Clocking Numbers

Clocking numbers instead of colors requires an infinite degree of patience, a larger betting stake, and more time. A partner is essential because the wheel may have to be watched for days to discern a pattern. Biases for one particular number are far less obvious than for a color and can only be discovered after clocking thousands of plays. Initially you should look at the wheel carefully before sitting down to play. Is it a new wheel? Are there any signs of wear? Are there any visible flaws? If the wheel looks perfect, it may still be flawed, but the chances will be better at an older wheel. Before coming to the casino prepare clocking sheets to assist you in recording each number as it hits. Spend a couple of bucks and get the sheets mimeographed if possible. The sheets should have spaces to record the number of total plays and number of times each number hit. While you are clocking these numbers, also record the colors.

There may, after all, be no number bias on that wheel, but there might be a color bias. To discover a number bias, you should record at least ten thousand plays. This may seem like a lot—it is—but the wheel moves fast, and you should be able to finish the record in two days. If you are at a casino in Monte Carlo or some other European spot, you may not have to clock at all. There is a past performance sheet published in Monte Carlo that records the behavior of each wheel at most casinos. Buy the published charts and calculate which wheels offer the best possibilities for play. Then watch the wheels for a few hours yourself to see that the bias continues. Since all wheels pay off at $36 for one, any number will have to hit one out of every thirty-six times to break even. One out of thirty-five times will show a small profit of 2.86 percent. But the investment is much greater playing numbers—you simply need more money—or at least betting units to find out that small profit by hitting one out of thirty-five times. Because of that and because losing streaks could wipe you out, it is suggested that you do not accept for play any number that occurs less frequently than one in thirty-two times. Unless you have a great deal of money or a great deal of time, that 2.86 percent for one in thirty-five, or 2.94 percent at one in thirty-four, is cutting it a bit close. Accept one in thirty-three at Monte Carlo or single-zero casinos. This refers only to single-number biases. Some wheels will have a preference for a series of numbers. If there is a warpage in the base or an irregular size fret, this could cause several adjacent numbers to come up with a frequency greater than probability. This may call for a four-number or six-number instead of a single-number bet. Take this six-number series for example: red *18*, black *31*, red *19*, black *8*, red *12*, black *29*. You have recorded 3,800 turns of the wheel. Each is likely to turn up one hundred times; red *18* has turned up 120 times, black *31* has occurred 135 times, red *19*, 118; black *8*, 117; black *29*, 100; and red *12*, 97. The numbers should hit six hundred times; they have hit 687 times. What's more, the first four numbers, which should have hit four hundred times, have hit 490.

The six numbers should hit 6-38 or 15.9 percent; the four numbers should hit 4-38 or 10.5 percent. Instead the six numbers hit 18 percent and the four numbers 13 percent. Is this enough for a profit? On 3,800 plays, the four numbers hit a total of 490 times at an 8-1 payoff for $4410 if $1 was bet each time. The six-number series payoff is 5-1 or $4122 for 3,800 plays at $1. This is a 16 percent profit on the four-number series and an 8.47 percent profit on the six-number series.

Either would substantially beat the house advantage. Most wheels will not be this warped. But accept for play, however, any number series that hits six and two-third times in every thirty-eight plays. Accept any four-number series that hits four and one-half times in every thirty-eight plays. Accept a three-number series that hits three and one-half times in every thirty-eight plays and a two-number bet that hits two and one-fourth times for thirty-eight plays.

Avoid columns and group betting and even or odd, high or low. The chances of beating the wheel lie in other patterns, not these. In playing a number system, be careful not to blow all that painstaking clocking by dumb betting. Avoid progression systems and always bet the same amount on each wager. While you are clocking the wheel, the casino will require you to bet much of the time you are sitting before the wheel. So again, bet only the minimum amount and bet one color only. Do not switch colors; do not change the amount of your bet. This will minimize the cost of learning the idiosyncracies of the wheel.

A warning seems in order here. Once you have discovered the biases of the wheel, you still may not make that big killing you have always dreamed about. Your calculations could be faulty or incomplete. The casino could change or repair wheels on you. The ultimate defeat is when you have found the perfect wheel and are just beginning to win big, and the casino operators tell you to take your business elsewhere. The only way you can avoid this latter possibility is to stick to European casinos or look as inconspicuous as possible. Do not bet $1000 on every spin or someone is going to notice you. Casinos in the United States and South America, particularly, only like high rollers who lose. For the serious roulette player, stick to Europe, preferably Monte Carlo. The odds are better and these places are less likely to throw anyone out for winning, reasoning that an occasional big winner is good publicity for the casino. In fact, some of these casinos will provide pencil and paper for you to make your calculations. And, as mentioned before, you can purchase roulette past performance sheets in Monte Carlo— recordings of the behavior of each wheel in certain casinos.

But even with the danger from casino operators, it is possible to win at roulette if you reduce the chances against you by learning the number and/or color patterns of a certain wheel. If you do not have the time or the inclination to catch idiosyncracies, then set a limit on the amount of money you are willing to lose and once it is lost, get out.

The casual bettor may just be playing roulette until the crap table crowd thins out or is just resting his or her feet. For this bettor, play numbers instead of colors or any of the even odds bets. If you are only going to play for a short time, play for the big odds rather than the minor profits. But limit your bets to small amounts and get out once you have lost it.

126

OTHER CASINO GAMES

In the Nevada casinos, there is a vast array of other games of chance available to the unwary sucker. These include keno, chuck-a-luck, slot machines, and various wheels of fortune. None of these games are at all recommended; the house advantage on each is unbeatable and, in some cases, totally absurd.

Take keno, for example. The bettor may be attracted by the promise of high payoffs, but at no time will he ever get a payoff closely approximating the actual odds of the bet. The top payoff in keno is $25,000, yet the odds of winning the top payoff are about nine million to one. The fairest bet in keno carries a house advantage of "only" 20 percent.

Fortune wheels also carry at least a 20 percent house advantage. Slot machines vary according to machine and casino but range upward to 50 percent. Chuck-a-luck is relatively fair compared to these—the house cut is only 7½ percent.

Chuck-a-luck

Chuck-a-luck is another dice game, though it is not related to craps. Three dice are shaken up in a fully enclosed cage. The cage twirls around on an axle and when it stops, the three dice rest on the bottom of the cage. The sides of the three dice pointing up are the points. The bettor wagers that one of the six numbers (1, 2, 3, 4, 5, 6) will appear on at least one of the dice. If one die shows the number wagered, the player is paid off at even money; if two dice show the number wagered, the player is paid off at 2-1; if all three dice come up the player's number, the payoff is 3-1.

Most players figure that because there are six num-

127

bers and three dice that the bet is fair. This assumption is false. Mathematically the house has a 7½ percent edge. Consider that there are 216 possible combinations or ways to throw those three dice (6 × 6 × 6, since each of the die must be considered separately and multiplied by the number of sides on each succeeding die). Yet if your number is six, for example, there is only one way to roll that three-figure combination. To get the single number, it is necessary to note that there are five ways to roll another number and only one way to roll yours on every roll of the dice. The chances against on this can be expressed as $5/6 \times 5/6 \times 5/6 = 125:216$. This is hardly an even bet. Again, if your number is six, there are a limited number of ways of hitting that particular pair and the odds against you are greater than 2-1. Thus, chuck-a-luck is a losing game for the gambler.

Wheel of Fortune

The wheel of fortune, or Big Six, uses a wheel instead of dice. The same six numbers are available in three number combinations on the wheel. You bet one number; if it matches one number on the combination that shows up on the wheel, you get paid off at even odds; two numbers pays 2-1; three numbers 3-1. There are on the standard Big Six wheel fifty-four sections: six no-pair combinations, twenty-four combinations, and twenty-four three-of-a-kind combinations. Since there are more high-payoff combinations, it would seem that Big Six might have an advantage to the player. But the house advantage is over 20 percent.

In the six no-pair combinations, there is a total of eighteen numbers, thus each individual number (1−6) will show up three times. The payoff is even and the chances are even. In the twenty-four pair combinations, each number will show up as the pair four times, or one out of every six pair combinations. On these pair combinations, each number will win an additional four out of eighteen even odds bets since the wheel combinations are three digit; the twenty-four pair combinations will leave an extra number; each number will appear four times as this extra number. In the twenty-four triples, each number will show up four times, again for a one in six chance.

Consider you are betting $1 on the number six on each spin for fifty-four spins and each combination on the wheel hits once—or its exact chance of hitting. This is what should occur: six is even on the single number combinations. Bet $6; three wins at even odds equals $6. On the double combinations, six pays off $3 each time it hits on a $1 bet. There are twenty-four combinations for a $24 investment, six hits four pairs for a $12 return and four singles for $8. The total received on pairs is $20, for a $4 deficit. On the triple bet, six again hits four out of twenty-four times on a $24 investment, a 3-1 payoff returns $16 for an $8 deficit. Your total overall investment is $54. Total loss is $12 for a 22.2 percent house advantage. There is no way to beat this kind of cut. Avoid the game.

Other wheels of fortune offer different payoffs and a greater or lesser number of combinations, but the principle is the same. The house allows for at least a 20 percent cut. Since wheels of fortune are mechanical, certain numbers could come up more often than others because of flaws in the wheel. But it is not worth trying to catch those flaws. A gambler has to have an edge. If a wheel were flawed more than 20 percent, management would have cast it aside long ago.

Keno

Wheels of fortune and chuck-a-luck are pikers compared to keno. As already mentioned, the top payoff is an attractive $25,000 but the odds on hitting it are astronomical. Keno is a game similar to bingo. There are eighty numbered ping-pong balls put in a cage. Twenty of those balls are drawn from the cage. You select ten numbers. If all ten numbers are among those selected you win $25,000, for a $2.50 ticket. If nine numbers show up, you get paid at a rate of 2,800 to one, yet the chances are one in 160,000. If five numbers hit, you get paid off at 2-1 on a 20-1 shot.

There are a number of other bets, but none approach a reasonable payoff for the bettor. Also, that $25,000 big payoff is the maximum allowed for all winners in a game. Anyone who hits the big payoff has to share it with lesser winners. If, for instance, two players each have hit all ten numbers, they split the $25,000—so the odds are reduced even further by the chances of the other players in the game. Avoid Keno. It is a stupid game.

Slot Machines

Slot machines are in casinos, airports, restaurants, all over the gambling towns of Nevada. Slots pay off on certain combinations of figures showing up in the window. Payoffs can range from a few nickels to $10,000 or more. Machines operate on any kind of American coin, though payoffs, of course, are higher for the higher coin machines. Slots are one of the biggest money makers for the casinos since their cut is not regulated. The cut varies from machine to machine, casino to casino, from 10 or 20 percent to 50 or even 90 percent. A group of gamblers discovered a way to beat the slots back in the 1950s. It was called the Rhythm Method and the gamblers took advantage of flaws in the slot machines. By pulling the handle down at a certain point in the spin of the slot rolls, the

"Rhythm" boys could beat the slots. Those flaws have since been corrected, however, and the chances for great riches on this account have long since passed.

Slots cannot be beaten, but they are fun to try. If you play the slots, set a limit on your losses and once you have lost that, get out. Since some slots pay off more than others, you might watch some other players for awhile and then just play the machine that had the greatest percentage of winners. Machines that do not pay off after several hours of play are not due to win—they are rigged to lose—so avoid them.

THE NUMBERS

The numbers game is a multi-billion dollar industry in the United States. It started in the black ghettoes of the north but has been taken over by the Mafia in a number of bloody battles over the past four decades. The game is incredibly profitable—for the people who run it. For the people who play it, it is a cheap bet with the promise of a big payoff. The numbers bet pays off at 599 to one and the minimum bet is sometimes as low as 5 cents. But like all games of chance, the payoff is not justified by the chances of winning.

In this game you bet any three-digit number as that particular day's number. If it comes in you get $600 for every $1 bet. But there are one thousand available numbers (000 to 999), so the house advantage is a whopping 40 percent. Considering that $5 to $10 billion is bet on numbers each year, no wonder the Mob fought to control the game.

While the Mob controls it, few bettors see any big mobsters when they make a numbers bet. The wagers are given to numbers "runners," who work for bookmakers or policy banks. (Policy is another word for numbers.) These runners are usually neighborhood people, not lower level criminals. The numbers runner is often well regarded around the neighborhood; he does favors for everybody while getting down their bets. In a hospital where the nurses were notably lax about seeing to patients' needs, the local numbers runner was taking orders for food, magazines, extra pillows, etc., when he made his daily rounds. You can also bet hunches with your bookie, but the majority of action is with the runners. Runners are the first to get hit in a police bust, but other than that it seems to be a good job. The runner gets paid by the bank or bookmaker taking his bets. And he gets 10 percent commission on whatever his customers win. This commission, of course, cuts down your payoff considerably, but on a 999-1 bet in which you are only receiving 599-1, what is 10 percent, more or less.

The number each day is usually selected from the last three figures in the total handle, or amount of money bet on all the races at that day's meeting at the local race track. Some policy banks have, at times, made up their own number out of thin air avoiding numbers that were getting play that day. But today the number is more randomly and honestly arrived at—there is no way anyone can manipulate that final number if it is the track handle.

Some numbers operators, however, will stiff you on certain numbers. Certain numbers generally get bigger play—today's date, 711, etc., so the bank will consider these cut numbers and pay off at only four hundred to one, although your chances of hitting have not changed one bit.

The numbers game is not in any way recommended as a serious bet. But if you just want to play around, take one number and always bet that number. Do not change because in last night's dream you are being chased by a bus and the dream book says this means number 342. Dream books are sold all over, promising to translate dreams into winning numbers. If the writers of these books really believed dreams predicted certain numbers, they would be spending most of their time sleeping instead of pushing these little books. You should not change your number because this is a strict luck bet, and the day you switch may very well be the day your original number comes in. Bookies claim that all their customers who bet this single number system hit at least once a year. But there are no assurances, bookies to the contrary, that your number will ever come up. Another way to bet is a combination number, say 123. This gets you 1,2,3; 2,1,3; 1,3,2; 2,3,1; 3,1,2; 3,2,1 or six possible numbers. Your chances are increased, but the payoff is reduced to one hundred to one.

The numbers game is for suckers and if you do bet it, never bet more than 50 cents or $1 per bet. Some gamblers have bet as much as $10,000 on a single number. This is just plain stupid. A person who plays numbers deserves everything he gets.

LOTTERIES

Lotteries are a new means for the average man or woman to get rich quick. For 50 cents or $2.50, or whatever, you can win up to $1 million and at the same time provide needed revenues to your state. The odds against winning the lottery are obviously much higher than the payoffs (the reason for the lottery, after all, is to provide a substantial profit for the state running it). There is no assurance that you will ever win even if you buy a ticket every week for the rest of your life. But the investment is small and the payoff is so attractive.

To increase your chances of winning the lottery it is recommended that you buy more than one ticket a week. The winners usually have bought at least five tickets per week. The multiple tickets give you a chance of winning at least something once a year,even if it's only $5 or five more tickets.

BINGO

Just about everybody knows how to play bingo. The standard bingo card has twenty-four numbers, the letters *B,I,N,G,O* on top, and a free space in the middle of the card. The numbers on the card correspond to seventy-five basic numbers. *B, 1—15; I, 16—30; N, 31—45; G, 46—60;* and *O, 61—75.* When a number is called, the player places a token over that number if it appears on his or her card. The first person to hit five numbers in a straight or diagonal line and shout "bingo," wins. Some games offer additional prizes for hitting corners or covering the whole card after the first legitimate "bingo" is achieved.

Bingo has been popularized as a gambling game by churches and charitable institutions. Lately, however, organized crime figures in certain cities have seen the potential profits in the game and are attempting to take over. Many of the legal, church, or charity-sanctioned bingo games are run by promoters who take a cut of the profits up to 90 percent. So if you are a bingo player, do not alibi your losses by saying you are losing the money to charity. For the most part, it just is not true any more. Some cheaper casinos in Nevada also run bingo games; these casinos do not even make any pretenses that they are financing good deeds. Bingo is a high-profit game and high-profit games are attractive to casinos.

In a standard bingo gambling game, the players "pay" for use of bingo cards and the winners receive a percentage of this sum received from them. The house cut is dependent on the bingo operator, but will usually be about 50 percent. This is a pretty stiff house advantage to be working against. If there are twenty players in the game, your chances of winning are one in twenty, but you will be paid at half that. Thus, in the long run you should expect a 50 percent loss at bingo. You may win because bingo is purely a game of chance. But hitting bingo is totally dependent on luck, and you have no sure way of changing the odds against you. There is one recommended way to increase your changes on a night's play: Buy more cards. By using three or four cards, you multiply your chances of winning because most numbers called will be on at least one of the cards. It will give you a slight edge over your opponents. But it does not improve your odds because you have to pay for the extra cards and each card has an independent chance of winning or losing.

Bingo is not a game to bet to make money. But if you are going to play, shop around for the places that offer the best prizes for the lowest investment—you might as well get something out of it if you do win.

4

Sports Betting

It has been estimated that over $50 billion each year is bet illegally on team sports, primarily football, baseball, and basketball. The sports betting end of gambling has perhaps the greatest growth potential. Hockey has just started its climb as a major nationwide gambling sport. Basketball betting has come back from its decline after the 1950s point-shaving scandals. Football betting is booming; every office has a football pool and football cards have become a national weekly fall ritual.

Sports betting is illegal everywhere but Nevada, although New York City's Off-Track Betting Corporation is trying to get in on the action. And in Michigan, lottery officials are testing the possibility of state-run football cards. With this increased interest in sports betting comes an increased need for knowledge by the average bettor on how to bet wisely.

All sports betting is currently conducted by bookmakers so the first step is to find a reliable bookie. If you do not know one, ask around. Someone you know is likely to have come in contact with a bookie at some time. Finding a bookie might be a harder task for a woman than a man. Men, after all, have been less protected from the criminal element. But it is interesting to note that there are an estimated 10,000 women bookies in the United States today, some of whom run multimillion-dollar betting shops. Do not do business with any bookie unless he or she comes recommended by a satisfied customer whom you trust. Bookies are, as a rule, extremely honest people. They have to be to stay in business. But there are a number of deadbeats. If, after using a bookie for awhile, he consistently offers you bad odds or poor point spreads, or he stiffs you on a payment, drop him. A bookie does not have to play his customers for suckers in order to make a profit.

Most bookies today are Mob-connected. This does not mean that they have guns and will rub you out if you fail to pay off. The Mob provides a back-up service so that if the bookie gets too much action on one team, he can "lay off" the bets with other Mob-connected bookmakers who have more action on the other team. The head "office" also provides cash for the bookmaker to pay off big losses in turn for a cut in the bookmaker's profits. Were it not for the services provided by organized crime, a lot of bookmakers would be in constant financial distress, not because bookmaking isn't a profitable enterprise—it is—but because on any given day, week, or month, a bookie can take a real beating. His profits even out over the year so the office is there to carry him through the bad spells.

Mob connections and bookies themselves conjure up visions of busted heads and arms. But bookies do not operate that way any more. First, before allowing a new customer to bet substantial amounts of money on credit, the bookie checks his credit. Then, if his credit is good, and the customer still finks out, the bookie will first try to get it from the customer, and failing that, will go to the customer's employer, trying to get the latter to garnishee the deadbeat's wages. The bookie will also cut off the bettor's credit and pass the word to other bookmakers who, in turn, will not accept that bettor's wagers. If the bettor is dumb enough to borrow money from a loan shark to pay the bookie and then cannot pay the loan shark, then he gets his head broken. But bookies are a peaceful lot.

In sports betting there are two standard kinds of line a bookie will quote for a bet. On hockey, baseball, and boxing the bet will be an odds bet. On football or basketball, the bet will involve point spreads. On football cards, the bet is an odds bet; you pick a certain number of winning teams for a particular weekend of football for a high odds payoff. But the odds offered are far less than justified by the chances of winning. Thus football cards should be avoided, and in this section only the point spread bets in football and basketball and odds bets in baseball, hockey, and boxing will be considered.

In all sports betting a line is set for betting on a game. Often that line is set by the legal, professional bookmakers in Las Vegas. The line may be adjusted by an individual bookmaker if he is getting too much action on one team. Thus, to make the other team more attractive to future customers, he will change the odds, offering a better profit or better spread for the team with little action. (Later revisions, however, will not change your bet. You get paid off at the odds that were prevelent when you made your bet; you win depending on the point spread at the time you made your bet.)

On an odds bet, you win if the team you bet on wins; you lose if your team loses. On a point spread bet, it is not enough to select the winner. On a football game, for example, a point spread bet might read like this: Vikings five over Jets. This means that for you to win your bet, the Vikings have to beat the Jets by more than five points. If you bet the Jets, you win if the Jets win or if the Vikings fail to cover the spread, a term meaning they won by less than five points. If the Vikings win by exactly five, the bet is off. To avoid this situation, games increasingly will have half-point spreads, such as Vikings five and one-half over Jets. Somebody wins; somebody loses.

You find out the line on today's or this week's games by calling your bookie. Ignore lines posted in the newspaper. You're not placing bets with a sports editor. If you are interested in one particular game or team over the others, do not tip your hand to the bookie. He may revise his line on the assumption that you are intending to bet a particular team. Do not say for instance, "What are the odds on the Yankee game?" The bookie knows you usually bet the Yanks. The odds are 6-5 "pick 'em" (which is an even bet), but you have tipped him off so he might up the odds on the Yankees to 6-7 over the other team, which means you're giving him 7-5 on your Yankees bet. You now bet $7 to win $5, instead of the 6-5 bet in which you bet $6 to get $5. Just ask for the complete line on the games, write down the prices, and say you will call back.

In sports betting the bookmaker always has an edge. An even bet is not an even bet. In football, for example, if you decide to take the Vikings over the Jets, and bet $100, if you win, the bookie pays $100; if you lose, you pay $110. (This applies no matter what side you bet.) In baseball an even game will be 6-5 or 5½-5 pick 'em, depending on how good a customer you are. It is supposed to be an even bet, but you do not get even odds no matter which team you choose. If it is 5½-5, it is the same as football. You bet $100 and get $100 if you win, and pay $110 if you lose. At 6-5, you pay $120 when you lose.

On the point-spread bets there is no way to get an edge over the bookmaker; it will never get above even odds. In the odds bets, if you bet the underdog, only then will the bookmaker pay you over even. For instance, the odds are Yanks 6-7 over Red Sox. Bet the Yanks and you give the bookie 7-5; bet the Red Sox and the bookie gives you 6-5.

If you want big payoffs, stick with horse racing or any of the other parimutuel games. In sports betting you have to bet big to win big. Bookies often set a minimum of $50 for sports bets—a far cry from the $2 minimum parimutuel ticket. But sports betting can be beat. The way to do it is by learning enough about a game so that you can spot flaws in the line or odds quoted. You have to bet the underdog in the odds betting when you feel the team's chances are better than the oddsmaker anticipates. You have to be able to make your own point spreads in football and basketball or you will only be betting your opinions against those of a professional, yet fallible, oddsmaker. Finally, sports betting can be beaten on the college level, in football and basketball, because you can, with a little bit of work, know more about a certain game or team than a Las Vegas oddsmaker who is required to set point spreads for 150 different games.

The following sections contain a formula for making your own point spreads for betting pro-football and basketball; a new updated method of betting baseball; and tips on betting college football and basketball, professional hockey, and boxing.

BASEBALL

Baseball has gone through a number of transformations since its initial growth as a professional, national pastime—from dead ball to live, from a hitter's game to a pitcher's game, from all-white to integrated, from offensive to defensive. Fifty years ago the game was a hitter's paradise. Pitching was unsophisticated, ballparks small, and fielder's gloves little more than padding for their hands.

Today dozens of regular professionals struggle to hit .230; a man with a .300 average is considered superstar material. Pitchers are developed and coddled from childhood on; in Little League it is usually the biggest, most physically mature kid who gets to pitch. For the past twenty years at least the pitcher has been the prima donna of baseball and he is the one who determines the betting odds in baseball games.

When a bookie quotes you odds on a baseball game, he is giving odds on the pitchers, not the teams. A late switch of pitchers and the bet is off (unless you agree in advance to continue the bet at whatever odds the bookie revises on the new pitcher).

A bet on baseball is a straight odds bet with the bookie getting his edge by offering uneven odds. For example, on a game considered even, the line might read Yankees 6-5 Detroit, pick 'em. This means on either bet you will wager $6 to win $5 (for a total payoff of $11). If his book is balanced (an equal number of bets on each team), the bookie will receive $1 profit for each $12 wagered ($12 bet, $11 returned). This percentage is called "vigorish" and it is what keeps the bookie's kids in college.

A bookie offers two betting lines—one for his nickel-and-dime bettors, another for high rollers. The cheap line offers a 20-cent spread between payoffs; the better line is called a "nickel" or inside line, though the betting spread is actually 10 cents.

The 20-cent spread is indicated in the above example: You would be betting $1.20 to win $1. The inside line would be 5½-5 pick 'em or $1.10 to $1. This cuts the bookie's "vig" in half and is of great advantage to a bettor, but the bookie will only offer it for steady customers.

If a game is not even, the line might read something like Yankees 7-8 over A's. What this means is that if you bet the Yankees, you bet $8 to receive $5. If you bet the A's you bet $5 to receive $7. All odds listed in the bookie's line are to the number five: bet the underdog and the bookie gives you the odds to five; bet the favorite and you are giving the bookie odds to five. In the above example, if it is a balanced book, the bookie will root for the underdog because he receives $8 but only has to pay off $7. If the favorite wins, he breaks even—paying and receiving $5.

Books are rarely balanced, however, and baseball betting is one of the easiest gambling games to beat, so a lot of bookies start to cringe when baseball season comes around. Bookies often take a beating on baseball and only accept the action to keep their more lucrative football bettors happy.

Bookies may be taking a beating because the morning line does not take into account the latest transformation in baseball. Pitching has become so uniformly superb and the pitcher so essential to a team's defense that to beat a top pitcher, they have to run around him. Every major league has at least one top starter, sometimes two or more, and a good reliever or two. The development of pitching and refinement of fielding practically stopped the offensive attack of most baseball teams. So most managers and batters began to stress the long ball. (A home run could save the game.) Thus batters, and their teams, tried to model themselves after the old New York Yankees, ideally breaking up games with superior shows of power. But nobody's the old New York Yankees anymore—not even the New York Yankees. The pitching was too good or the hitters too untalented, and at any rate a pitcher's performance was still predictable. On the average, if he was good he would overpower the hitters. The hitters' strategy was to then play a waiting game with the pitcher. The batter stood at the plate and waited for the pitcher to make a mistake. If he got on base he waited for the pitcher to make another mistake. If he made enough mistakes, it was called a rally. This constant waiting only reinforced the importance of the pitcher. And it drove fans away by the millions. Left-on-base statistics reached double figures for single games.

The excitement of the game was gone; nobody was forcing anything to happen. All the batters were waiting, praying for the pitcher to collapse and too frequently, for the fans, it just did not happen.

The batters, and baseball managers in general, were always counting on luck to pull them through. With most of these pitcher—batter duels, a home run was nothing but luck—the pitcher letting one get away, the batter meeting the ball just right, in a direction where it would fall neatly over a wall.

So, betting on the pitcher was the only smart way to bet; and it was the only sensible standard for a betting odds line. A pitcher tended to pitch his game, whether good or bad, time and again. Pitchers were consistently good, bad, or average. A good pitcher would usually beat a bad or average one; it was something you could count, or bet, on.

Finally, some clever managers saw a way out. If the pitcher was not going to collapse, then they had got to get their runs in another way. The theory resulting from this is often labeled "building a run," an old concept inadequately used in the past thirty years. But it must be stressed that there are several ways of creating runs out of little or nothing. The better teams have fully developed their running attacks—base stealing, squeeze plays, hit and run plays, stretching out hits, etc. Other teams still pay only lip service to the concept.

The standard method for the old-fashioned lead-footed teams is to bunt a player from first to second, sacrificing an out to get the player in scoring position, then waiting for a hit. Note again the waiting. But a top running-team can score without a hit by stressing the base stealing of its runners. The Oakland A's are the top team in baseball today because of their running game. Their pitching is fine, but it is the running attack that breaks open games. If a player reaches first and is a threat to steal, this puts a strain on the opposing team's defense. The first baseman has to stay closer to the base than he would wish, likewise the second baseman. This creates a greater hole between first and second for the next hitter. The pitcher's concentration is split between the batter and the runner. Each time that runner makes a feint to second, anytime the pitcher starts thinking about him instead of the batter, that pitcher may make a mistake. The old method was to wait for mistakes. The new way is to force mistakes, and it has added a new dimension in handicapping baseball.

Interestingly enough, the "new way" is closer to the way baseball used to be played. Before Babe Ruth, no one counted on the home run; the offensive attack was far more varied. Now, the speed element has become particularly important if you are rating pitchers of seemingly equal ability. The odds may be even; the pitchers may both be in top condition. But the team whose offensive attack does not rely on the collapse of a consistent hurler is the probable winner.

How can you tell if a team has speed? Keep records

for the first few weeks of the season on the number of bases stolen by each team, number of attempted steals, the number of players who are base-stealing threats on each team, how often the team pulls hit-and-run or squeeze plays, how often a team's batters hit into double plays, and average number of men left on base per game. Do not bet at the beginning of any season—pitchers and teams have not settled well enough to be predictable. These records should hold for the season; only record again if a team changes managers.

It must be stressed here that the pitcher is still the single most important individual in the game. But to handicap a game it is essential to know the factors that will defeat a pitcher. Team speed can defeat a top pitcher in a game that is expected to be low-scoring between two pitchers of more or less equal ability. Even a great pitcher, after all, cannot be expected to throw a no-hitter every game—somebody's boing to get on base. Speed can throw off a pitcher—making a seemingly equal situation unequal. There are other effects on the outcome, however. Those other factors, how they can affect a game, and how to assess them in terms of betting, follow.

Pitcher's style and record: Favor a low-ball or control pitcher over a fast-ball pitcher. The control pitcher, when he is right, rarely makes mistakes. The fast-ball pitcher is more likely to serve a good pitch. Low-ball pitchers rarely give up home runs when they are pitching well, but do not count on this type of pitcher if his infield, through injuries or whatever, is sloppy. Those grounders and low liners will get through and the necessary double plays will not be made. Stealing will also increase.

As for a pitcher's record, pay attention both to Earned Run Average and Won-Lost Average. Both are essential in determining whether one pitcher and his team can beat another pitcher and his team. If one pitcher has a 14-14 record and a 2.65 ERA, and the other is 16-5 with a 3.87 ERA, go with the latter pitcher everytime. Go with success; the other pitcher is obviously good, but his team is not giving him any support.

Total defense: If the pitchers are equal, favor a team with a solid infield over an inexperienced, sloppy one. The reasoning here is that the infield is essential to the defense; if it is bad, the game will get out of hand. If one team has good base speed and the other team has a catcher with a sore arm, watch out for the former team, even if its pitcher is not quite as good. One or two base runners and the game could break open. As for the outfield, there is a great deal of uniformity in fielding ability and it should not play a part in handicapping a game.

Relief pitching is also an essential part of the defensive game. A bad relief staff means the starters have to stay in longer and the relievers will lose games rather than save them. Since there is such a reliance on relief pitchers now, watch out for any team without at least one top reliever.

Total offense: This includes hitting and running. If the pitchers are equal, the running game is equal, and the defense is equal, favor the team with the better batting average. Generally, the team that hits more often will win. Not always, but the law of averages is with you if you bet that way. If the pitchers are unequal and the team with the inferior pitcher has a better hitting and running game, these will even out the game. Yet the odds will probably be something like 7-8 favoring the team with the better pitcher. By betting the underdog, you can get 7-5 on an even bet. Bet it.

Team standings and records: A team in contention for the conference title will play harder than a team in contention for the cellar. This only applies to situations in which the final league standings are still in doubt. Once a team has won the conference flag by mathematically eliminating the other teams, it may dog it a bit. A lesser team will get fired up at the prospect of beating the top team. This, combined with the best team relaxing before the playoffs, makes the worse team dangerous. This factor is sometimnes known as the "salary drive switch." Disregard all other factors and bet the underdog.

Losing streaks: Both teams and pitchers will get into losing streaks. A pitcher in a bad streak will be the underdog, no matter how good his team is. If his team is still better than the other team, if he would normally be favored over the opposing pitcher, and the losing streak is not injury-related, bet him. Avoid teams on losing streaks, however. A real tail-spin adds an unknown factor, and you should only bet known quantities.

Overall a system for betting baseball should include the following rules:

1. If the pitchers are equal, bet the team with the best running game.
2. If one pitcher is better than the other, but the lesser pitcher is still competent, bet the team with the best running game.
3. If the teams are equal but one pitcher has a better record, bet the team with the better pitcher.
4. If one pitcher is bad, but has a good offense behind him, and the other pitcher is good but his team's offense is bad, bet the underdog. The chances are even, so take the higher odds.
5. If the pitchers and offensive teams are relatively equal, bet the team with the best relief pitching.

In general, never bet a favorite in baseball betting. You are risking too much to get too little. Also, never bet your hometown team; emotions can play in your assessment of each team. Never bet your hopes. Only bet in these situations:

1. The bookie's odds are even (6-5, or 5½-5 pick 'em), yet you favor one team.
2. The team you feel has the best chance of winning is the underdog.
3. According to your knowledge of the teams, the game is even but one team is favored. (Bet the underdog.)

In this latter situation the reasoning is that each team has an equal chance of winning the game. If it really is even, in situations like this over hundreds of games, the favorite will win half the time, the underdog the other half. Betting the favorite will result in a net loss. In a 7-8 odds game, for example, you receive only $5 when you win and pay $8 when you lose. While on the outsider you receive $7 when you win and pay $5 when you lose. Even if the underdog wins less than 50 percent of the time, you wind up with a profit.

Handicapping playoff or World Series games is the same as handicapping regular season games, only more so. All the playoff teams will likely have good pitching, both teams should have good hitting, so the running game looms very large—at least it has in recent playoffs and World Series games. In the 1972 American League playoff between Detroit and Oakland, for example, those lead-footed Tigers never had a chance. The last Tiger to steal bases was Ty Cobb. The Tigers went down the tube, content to take their revenge by throwing passing baseballs at the head of the A's top thief Bert Campaneris.

The A's did it again in the 1973 World Series against a fine defensive club with some of the best pitching in baseball, the New York Mets. If the pitching is good, if the teams are good enough to get to the playoffs or World Series, bet the team that can force mistakes over the team that waits. In the playoff or World Series situation, bet the speed team as the overall winner, and bet the individual games only if your team is the underdog or the odds are even.

FOOTBALL

Football is not an easy game to play or to bet. Too many gamblers get sidetracked by the high-payoff football cards. Yet the payoffs on these multigame parlays are never anywhere near the odds of winning. Straight bets are more profitable in the long run, but even the straight bet is a double killer. Picking a winner is not enough; you have to predict by how many points a team should win. Even then, you never get an edge; the bet is considered even, but you have to bet $110 to win $100, no matter which team you play. If the game is Jets six over Miami and you bet the Jets, you win only if the Jets win by more than six. If you bet Miami, you win if Miami wins or if the Jets win by less than six points—exactly six and the bet is off.

The smart gambler only bets football when he thinks there is a discrepancy in the game line. If the Jets are favored over Miami by six points, for example, never bet if this line seems fair or nearly fair. If indeed the Jets should win over the Dolphins by six points, do not bet either team. The six-point spread equalizes the teams; if the spread correctly assesses the relative abilities of the two teams, then the person who bets the Jets plus six and the person who bets the Dolphins each have an equal chance of winning the bet. But because the payoff is less than even, or 11-10 against, the risk is unwise. If you continue to bet in this type of situation, you will, on the average, win half the time since your chances are 50-50 based on hundreds of plays, but you will wind up losing, overall, $1 for every $12 bet, or exactly the amount of the bookmaker's commission on football bets, 8⅓ percent.

Instead, you have to beat the line. You have to find flaws in it, and the flaws have to be enough to counter that 8⅓ percent house take. A one-point discrepancy is not enough; four points or more is essential. This is not at all easy, particularly in pro-football. Bookies generally use a Las Vegas line; the Las Vegas linemaker has access to injury reports, weekly statistics, personnel information, and team records against each possible opponent. The linemaker is not likely to make many mistakes in pro-football; the spot is covered too heavily by the news media for you to be privy to inside information that he does not know about. This is not to say that he cannot be wrong. Upsets are frequent in the National Football League. But, in order to tell if the line is wrong, you have to keep close track of all the news about each pro team and you should be able to make your own point spreads (more about this later).

College Football

You stand a much better chance of beating the point spread in college football. On any given Saturday, the linemaker will rate up to 150 games, some of them major rivalries, or otherwise between major teams. These games, since the bulk of betting will occur on them, get the greatest attention. These point spreads will more closely approximate the real abilities of each team. But the linemaker cannot be equally knowledgeable about all 150 games. If you take a smaller conference (not the Big Ten, for example) and make it a point to study those teams, you may be able to pull off a betting coup.

First, get subscriptions to the college papers and the local college town newspapers covering the teams in your selected conference. These papers will more thoroughly cover the problems of the local football team than a larger newspaper that saves most of its space for professional sports. Second, in considering which conference to study, avoid colleges where there is not at least some "rah-rah spirit." Otherwise those media sources might be terribly limited. Keep a record of injuries to key players, turnovers from year to year, any extenuating circumstances that might cause an essential player to make mistakes in a game (such as family or scholastic problems, recent arrests, etc.). Much of this information may not get to the linemaker in time for it to affect his game line, and you can beat the point spread if you know more about the teams than the linemaker. But again, once you have this information, if it just confirms that the given line is close to correctly rating the two teams, do not bet. Only bet if one of the teams is at least four points better than its rating.

A final word on college football. Do not study or bet a college you attended. You may be betting your opinions and that is a bad practice. It is also important to remember that college teams can change greatly from year to year. Some colleges win year in and year out, but others go through cycles. You might assume that studying a conference you know something about (via your attendance at one school in that conference) will give you an advantage. But instead, you will likely rate the teams by preconceived notions, affected by emotions and what happened five or ten years ago. It is better to start from scratch and study the teams of a conference for several games into the season before making your first college bet.

To narrow down possible conferences or groups of

teams to study, keep records of which teams seem to upset the point spread more often. If a number of teams that
often play each other get on your upset list, start watching
them; you may have hit the linemaker's weak spot. As for
post-season bowl games—do not bet them. The teams
have not faced each other and usually have not had one
common opponent for the previous season; thus they cannot be sufficiently compared.

Professional Football

The key to winning at professional football is to de-
vise your own point spreads, compare them with your
bookie's line, and then do not bet unless there is a discrepancy of at least four points between your figures and
his. To arrive at your own point spread you will have to
compare each team according to its current record; its
finish last year; personnel problems or injuries; quality of
quarterbacl, kicker, total defense, and total offense. To
predict what a team will do in the future you have to look at
the past. Formulas for determining the point spread are
given in the following sections.

Base score. Take last season's statistics for total
points scored and scored against. Get an average per game
figure for both teams. Subtract the points-against average
from the points-for figure. This is the base number for
each team. The base score is a reflection of each team's
total offense and total defense. The average total of points
scored per game indicates the ability of the running backs,
blockers, kickers, ends, quarterback, the whole offensive
attack.

Quarterback. If a team has a superior quarterback,

one who is statistically always at the top of the league when he is healthy, give the team six points. For a good, reliable, but uninspired quarterback, give it three points. For a poor quarterback, subtract three points.

Extra consideration should be given, however, to the quarterback because in pro-football he is such an essential part of the team's offense; it just does not move without him. A rotten quarterback is going to cost his team dearly, just as a spectacular quarterback can make at least a touchdown's difference in the final score of the game. Good quarterbacks can also be relied on to provide the required offensive punch. Consider a quarterback merely good if he is a threat as a passer or as director of the running game or within the top half of pro-quarterbacks statistically, but not in the top 10 percent. Consider a quarterback bad if he is in the bottom quarter statistically. This rating on quarterbacks implies that the man is healthy. Joe Namath, for example, deserves the extra six points and more when he is right. But when he is not, the offense falls apart and he plays terribly. If a quarterback is sour, or playing while injured, subtract three points. If he is right, add whatever is justified by his record.

Turnovers. Keep records on each team for the average number of turnovers (fumbles or interceptions) committed or forced each game. Subtract three points for each fumble or interception that the offense averages per game. But add three points for the average number of interceptions or fumbles recovered that defense commits per game.

The turnover score is a reflection of offensive and defensive balance. A sloppy team will continue to make mistakes and is at a particular disadvantage against a team with a solid record of interceptions and forced fumbles.

Forcing fumbles and picking off interceptions is a sign of an aggressive defense; the more such turnovers averaged per game, the more aggressive a team. If the opposing teams are unbalanced in this respect, it can easily affect the score and the outcome of the game.

Personnel changes. Subtract one point for each rookie in a starting or key defensive or offensive position. Subtract three points for each major player who has an incapacitating injury; subtract one point if the injury is merely serious enough just to slow him down. Subtract one point for each secondary player who has an incapacitating injury. Subtract two points for each major veteran who is no longer with the team through off-season retirement, trades, injuries, etc. Add two points for each solid veteran acquired via trades.

Finally, while the quality of teams, as a rule, does not change too drastically from year to year or within a season, substantial personnel changes can cause a team to prove an exception to that rule. These changes can be caused by retirement, injuries, trades, or just new faces in the lineup. But these will have bearing on any team's chances in the future.

Because of the rough nature of pro-football, players are getting injured all the time. Some injuries are bad enough to keep a player out of the game; others will merely make him a bit cautious or a little slower than usual. This has an effect on the way a team plays. For example, if Buffalo's O.J. Simpson were injured, that team's entire running attack would be devastated and the team would have to adapt to that loss. The running backs taking up the slack may be just as good, but the team will make mistakes anyway because it has been trained with O.J. as the key. Remove him and the team has to suffer.

155

If a key player is injured during the season, the effect can be worse because the team does not have as much time to adjust, thus the difference in points allotted for off-season injuries. If a key player is only slowed down, it will still change his team's chances. The other team may start running plays at him; or his team cannot use him as much as they need him. Both injury situations will put a stress on the other players who have to compensate for the loss, whether total or partial, of that key player.

Likewise if a secondary member of the team is injured, this sacrifices the depth of a team. The injury problem will be particularly acute from now on since the new NFL rules have cut down the number of players allowed per team and banned the taxi squads. If in the past a team had too many injuries it had enough players to fill the ranks from either its regular team lineup or the reserves. Those reserves will not be available anymore, starting in the 1975—76 season, so the teams with the healthiest players, rather than the teams with the best players, may wind up in the playoffs for the next few years.

The reason for subtracting points if a rookie is in the starting lineup is that rookies make mistakes and generally should be brought along slowly. When a team is forced to rely on a first-year man, no matter how talented, it is usually a sign of weakness. Football players grow into the National Football League.

Defense. Add one point for each blocked kick or safety achieved by the defense in the last six games.

Blocked kicks and safeties are signs of a superior defense, but usually will not occur often enough for most teams to get an average. If you only have the total season records for these feats and cannot get those for the past six games, cut the number in half and award that number of points for defense.

The kicker is also an essential offensive factor, despite the 1974 rule which put the goalpost ten yards in back of the goal line. Most kickers, to make it in pro-football, have to be fairly good. Some are unreliable. The unreliable ones will cost their teams at least one field goal per game, which is the reason for the subtraction on the point spread formula.

Previous placing. Add three points if the team reached the playoffs last season. Add an extra three points if the team led its conference at the end of regular season play. Subtract three points for any team that had a below .500 record in the previous year.

After the first six games of the season, not including exhibition games, use this season's statistics to get a base score. Stop giving points for last year's standings. Award three points to each team that is leading or tied for the lead in the current conference standings, and subtract three points for any team playing under .500. Stop awarding or subtracting points for off-season personnel changes.

The quality of a professional football team will not change greatly from year to year. Teams tend to build up and break down slowly. Thus, using last year's statistics and placings should give you a key to the possible outcomes of this year's games.

Once you've arrived at a point spread, only bet if there is a discrepancy of four points or more. You have to give yourself enough of an edge to wipe out the bookmaker's 8⅓ percent cut.

On playoff and Super Bowl games, do not try to figure out a point spread for the teams. If the teams have gotten that far, intangibles like heart and spirit will take over and you cannot give numeral scores to heart and spirit. As a rule, in post-season games, always bet the underdog. The games, even if one team seems touchdowns ahead of the other, will tend to be very close. Even if the favored team wins, the chance are good that it will not cover the point spread.

BASKETBALL

Baseball and football handicapping revolve around the theory of the essential man. While there are other factors involved, the outcome of the game relies heavily on either the quarterback or the pitcher. If the pitcher bombs out, the baseball team faces an uphill struggle. A weak or injured quarterback cripples a football team's offense and usually seals its doom.

But bettors will be making a mistake if they try to carry over that theory to basketball. The center is often the playmaker, or the chief rebounder or scorer, so it is assumed that superstar "big man" is in the same position as that of a pitcher or quarterback. But because of the nature of the game, an opposing team can stop even the greatest player by double-teaming him and working plays at the weaker players. The opposing team needs only to stop or slow down the superstar to control the game. Even a spectacular center cannot completely carry the team. A superstar can make a franchise, but he cannot necessarily guarantee that his team will win a particular game over a particular rival.

One man cannot win a basketball game (though he can shave enough points to keep the score down to cover the point spread). The team has to be reasonably well balanced. Weakness at any position can and will be exploited by the opposing team. The center must be able to set picks, rebound, and score. If he lacks any of these abilities the team will suffer. Too often the center is a hot scorer, but fails to play defense as well or fails to involve the other players in the total offensive game. This allows the opposing team to concentrate its defensive efforts against one man and can effectively limit a team's scoring punch. Likewise, the guards and forwards should be able to threaten the other team at both boards. A player who is not both an offensive and defensive threat can drastically affect the outcome of a game. The opposing team plays to that weakness, hitting that zone or man on offensive plays, ignoring him during defensive action. It is not like baseball where a team is willing to trade off some offensive punch for defense in certain positions.

There are only five players in basketball and the action is nonstop. An unbalanced team will be at the mercy of a balanced team and can lose even with superior personnel. The lack of balanced talent is what often characterizes the teams at the bottom of the standings in pro-basketball. Each team usually has at least one big superstar. But unless he has someone else of above-average ability to work with, struggle is all uphill.

Balance on the starting five is not enough. The team has to have some depth; the players on the bench must be able to play well enough so that the team does not collapse if a key player fouls out or tires or is injured in the game. Because of the foul-out rule, players can be forced to leave the game before the end. If the replacements are duds, the strategy is clear for the opposing team: Take out a troublesome player by forcing fouls on him, tiring him out by constantly running plays at him, or if the stakes are high enough and they're playing really rough, just physically knock him out of the game.

Some players have a greater tendency for fouling out. If a team's star or playmaker seems to end most games on the bench or in serious foul trouble, the team may have rough going against an opponent of seemingly equal or less ability. Even if the player does not ultimately foul out, from the time he receives his fourth foul, he will be forced to play a more cautious game to avoid elimination. A team with balance and depth will not be wiped out in this situation.

Relative balance and depth are major factors in handicapping basketball. But how can you tell which team has the greatest depth or which team is unbalanced? Watch the final scores of several games. How many players on each team will score in double figures in an average game? If it is four or more, the team is well balanced offensively. As for defense, do any one or two players have a prohibitive lead in rebounds? Does it appear that most of the players are not getting into any action at all under the boards? The team may not be balanced defensively. As for depth, look at each player's record for points, assists, and rebounds. How far ahead of the rest of the team is the starting five in each category. If they do not have much of a lead, and in fact several other players are equal or fairly close, the team has depth. It must be stressed, however, that this only indicates quality and balance compared to the other members of the team.

Yet balance and depth are the major measures of the relative strength of the two teams. The bookie's line on basketball games is based on the past: primarily standings, won-lost records, and previous games between the two teams. Examining personnel problems is the prime way of finding discrepancies in the bookie's point spread—which is the only way of beating basketball.

Injuries are another determinant of depth. An injury

that incapacitates or even slows down any player cuts the team's depth drastically. If the team loses a key player, the balance is affected, and possibly the outcome of the game.

There are other factors, however. These include playing style, home-court advantage, and average turnovers per game. The latter refers to the average number of times per game that a team either steals the ball or retrieves a rebound after the opposing team has attempted to score. Balance the number of times a team loses the ball in this manner against the number of times it gains the ball this way. A team with a high-gain average indicates an aggressive defense; a high-loss average indicates a sloppy offense.

Playing style is related to game strategy. Each team tries to force the other team to adopt its own playing style. A defensive team, by slowing down a running team, hopes to throw if off balance and keep it from breaking open the game. A fast-break team, however, forces mistakes on playmaking or defensive teams by not giving these teams enough time to set up offensive or defensive plays. It might appear that a fast-break team would have an advantage, but pay attention to propensities to foul and to injuries. This type of team particularly relies on depth, or the better players will run out of gas long before the end of the game.

To tell what type of playing style a particular team plays, watch a few games first before betting. The defensive teams will tend to be in low scoring games and will have a low scoring and scored-against average. The playmaking teams will find the center passing off frequently, setting picks, and slowing down the game a bit, but not nearly as much as the defensive team. These scores and averages will be somewhat in the middle. The running teams are easy to tell. They are the teams that fancy the fast break and constant movement and are characterized by high-scoring games.

Finally, in basketball the home-court advantage is significant. The basketball crowd is younger, more vocal, and more loyal than the football crowd. The games are not usually nationally televised, so the players are far less blasé about the home crowd's feelings. The fans are physically closer to the players and a certain almost-electrical current seems to pass between fan and player during particularly close games. So do not ignore this factor. Some teams rarely lose on their home court.

These are the factors that can determine the winner of a basketball game. But in betting basketball, you have to worry about a point spread. Picking winners is relatively easy. In betting the point spread, a standard line might be given as New York Knicks three points over Boston Celtics. This means that the Knicks not only have to win, but they have to beat the Celtics by more than three points—less than three points or a loss, and a bet on the Celtics will win. If the margin of victory is exactly three points, the bet is canceled. The odds are always 5½-5, which means you get $10 for every $11 bet. Many bookies set a bottom limit on sports betting. The minimum bet may be $50, which really means you bet $55 and the bookie pays off at $50.

How do you determine whether the point spread quoted by the bookie is beatable? If it only indicates the real abilities of the two teams, there is no reason to bet. You are just guessing. But the point spread may overlook a factor. By creating your own point spread for each game, you may be able to beat basketball.

To determine if the point spread is fair, use the following formula. To get the base number, subtract each team's points-against average from its points-for average, using last year's records or the totals from this season's games to date (if they have each played at least seven regular season games). These records are available in the sports pages of most daily newspapers; for last year's records, you might have to go to a library for back issues.

Take each team total as the starting point in determining a point spread. Give two points to a team that reached the playoffs, one additional point to the team that led the conference at the end of the regular season or won the conference title in the playoffs (one point maximum allowed). After the first quarter of the season is over, use the current standings, awarding two points to teams in playoff contention and one additional point to conference leaders.

For the first quarter of the season, subtract one point for each key player lost to the team by injury, trade, or retirement over the off-season. Subtract two points for any player lost through incapacitating injury during the regular season. Subtract one point for each first-year player in the starting five. Subtract two points for each player in the starting five who is either slowed up by injury or is weak on defense or offense. Add two points for home-court advantage. Subtract one point for each key player who fouls or gets in foul trouble in at least 40 percent of the games. Add two points for the team with the most aggressive defense. Add two points if the team uses a fast-break game.

All of the aforementioned factors will affect the total offense or defense of each team, resulting in lost or gained points. The final difference in points is the logical point spread. When you get the final totals, only bet those teams that either get a small point-spread advantage in your figures, yet are underdogs in the bookie's line, or get a

163

significantly larger point-spread advantage in your figures, yet are barely favored or considered even in the bookie's line. This will limit your bet to solid overlays; the closer your figures come to the bookie's line, the more the game should be avoided. Another word of advice from some professional basketball bettors: Never bet on your home team. Even if you think you are being perfectly objective, the chances are you will bet your emotions. Just avoid the game altogether.

There is a new bet in basketball called the "over and under bet." Each basketball game, in addition to the point spread, is now assigned a point total. This is the total number of points likely to be scored by both teams in that game. This line is made up either in Las Vegas or your bookie's home office (most bookies are not independent entrepreneurs but are Mob-connected). If the Knicks are playing the Boston Celtics, for example, the line might be 210 points. You bet that the total score will be over or under that number. At 210, the bet is canceled. The bet is called an even bet, but the odds are 5½-5, no matter which side you bet. Thus the odds are the same as for a point-spread bet, though it is certainly harder to hit for the casual bettor. The number is set according to what the two teams should score based on their playing styles and previous games against each other. The bet only becomes feasible if you can find a significant discrepancy in the bookmaker's line. The discrepancy would have to be ten points or more to limit the element of chance and give you a reasonable edge. This is not a recommended bet.

College Basketball

The recommendation here is the same as in college football. The Las Vegas linemaker cannot know 150 teams equally well. You can get an edge if you study a certain conference or group of teams that regularly play each other. (It is essential that the teams studied play each other; otherwise you will be running into unknown teams all the time.) Do not bet if the point spread seems fair, i.e., if you agree with its assessment of the two teams' relative ability. The bet is an even bet at less than even prices; you should not bet unless the chances of your winning can compensate for the bookie's percentage. Only bet if you see a decided edge—if the underdog is equal to or better than the favorite or if a lukewarm favorite is really drastically better than the underdog.

College basketball, it must be noted, is the easiest type of sports betting to fix. One player can easily shave points without being the least bit obvious. The temptation must be very great for athletes with little money and no hopes of making it to the pros. Shaving points is the only means available for making a substantial amount of money playing basketball. When the temptation, and the payoff, outweigh the risks, certain athletes are going to cheat. There is no way you, as a bettor, can guard against it. Just be wary of any college or professional team that consistently fails to cover its point spread when favored. Whether through deceit or simple failure, it is a good idea to avoid betting on or against such teams.

BOXING

Boxing continues its decades-long decline. The old days, when hundreds of boxers in every class fought each week, have long gone. Today the public avoids all but the heavyweight or championship fights. The fight game used to rival horse racing for the bulk of the gambler's dollar. Millions of dollars changed hands after the big fights. Today, it is a grimy sport full of losers making one-night stands, with only a few sleek fighters at the top to spur the dregs on to promised glory.

It has been said that television killed boxing. But that is only part of it. Boxing has always been a game of the poor financed by the very rich; its popularity waned with increased American affluence. Boxers always came from the lower classes; so did many fans who could identify with a fighter's struggle both inside and outside the ring. Neighborhoods and nationalities supported fighters; boxing was a symbol and ethnic boxers were heroes. Once the middle class began to dominate American life, boxing started on its way out. Fewer people identified with a poor kid from the slums, and the sport, being less personalized, was dropped in favor of newer, more upper class diversions. The current recession may see an upsurge of interest in boxing, but television now supplies the average American with cheap, violent thrills. People no longer have to go out of the house to see somebody's head bashed in.

As a result the number of professional fights has decreased. The class fights are becoming rare, so the opportunity to bet is fairly limited. Bookies will not take bets on boxing matches unless they are regularly sanctioned affairs put on by trustworthy promoters. Boxing has had so many fix scandals, even the bookies are wary. Today, however, there is such a diminished interest in the sport, the crooked gambler can only hope to make money off a fix on a championship or near championship fight. Fixes still occur, but the policing of boxing is so thorough today that a fix will rarely occur in a top level fight.

As for handicapping boxing, in general pay little attention to all those reach-weight statistics the newspapers and magazines publish just before a big fight. Boxing is not a Mr. Universe contest. Winning has more to do with strategy, coolness under fire, ability, and general condition than with measurements.

To handicap a boxing match, follow these rules:

1. Favor a boxer over a puncher.
2. Favor the champion over the contender, unless the champion is a puncher and has had a long layoff.
3. Favor a boxer who has fought recently over one who has had a long layoff.
4. Be wary of a fighter who is coming in five pounds or more over his best fighting weight.
5. In boxers under thirty years of age of seemingly equal styles and ability, favor the fighter with greater experience.
6. In fighters with similar fighting styles, favor the higher-ranked man.
7. In a fight between two punchers, favor the younger fighter as long as he is close in ranking to the older man.

The first rule is the most important, yet it is often overlooked by gamblers as well as fighters. There are two ways of winning a fight: by knockout or by points. The puncher is limited to knockouts if he is fighting a boxer. The boxer is going to look so good, the judges will be giving him points all over the place. A boxer is a fighter who uses the whole array of offenses and defenses available— he dances, feints, jabs, etc. The puncher is generally flat-footed and gets in a slugging exchange with his opponent. He is willing to take three punches to every one of his opponent's because he can take a punch and his hole card is that devastating, bone-crunching knockout punch. In a fight between two punchers, the best or sometimes the youngest man wins. In a fight between a boxer and a

167

puncher, those hard rights keep hitting the boxer's gloves or elbows, never connecting where they will do any harm. The puncher tires and the boxer, who also has a knockout punch, delivers it repeatedly against the sagging puncher's head. A perfect example of this type of fight was Muhammed Ali's victory over George Foreman.

A fighter has to be sharp against an opponent of relatively equal ability. Overweight or long layoffs will dull a fighter's form. A fat champion can beat a bum, as Muhammed Ali has proven, but his case is an exception. Do not expect it to happen with lesser fighters boxing men closer to their abilities. If boxers seem pretty close in ability, experience will tell, particularly in the later stages of a match. The inexperienced fighter tends to tire faster. Again, if the fighters seem equal on all counts, assume that the boxing publications know something and back the top-ranked fighter. Finally, a younger man, if he is even close in ability to the older fighter, should be able to take a punch better. The younger fighter between two punchers should prevail, but do not bet it unless the younger man is a quality fighter and has been hit by punchers similar to the man he is now facing.

The boxing bet is an odds bet. Always bet the best man. Since good boxing matches do not come along as often as they once did, it is difficult to wait around and only bet the underdog when you feel the young fighter has been favored. The odds will probably be close to each fighter's chances. But if you feel a fighter is too heavily favored, even though he is the best man, pass the bet. A 4-1 price, for example, on any boxer is ridiculous (betting $4 to get $1). It is not worth betting. If the fight is fairly equal, always bet the underdog. The bet has an edge. Accepting greater than even odds on an even bet will eventually wind up in a profit.

HOCKEY

Betting on hockey games has significantly increased over the past several years following the expansion of the old National Hockey League. For years the league had only six teams, two of which were Canadian, which certainly limited its growth as a gambling sport. Now there are two hockey leagues and expansions into cities that never saw ice before, much less a Canadian on ice skates. Hockey has been getting so popular with gamblers that the NHL has even hired security guards to protect the game from gambling incidents.

Yet hockey has a fairly clean past. Back in 1948 two players were suspended for life for betting on games. And six years ago, a timekeeper for the Montreal Canadiens was threatened with great bodily harm unless he rigged the clock. But these were certainly minor concerns compared to the 1919 Black Sox scandal or the college basketball point-shaving fixes that involved eighty-six games and thirty-six players between 1947 and 1950, and thirty-seven more players ten years later.

Like baseball and football, hockey has an essential man—the goalie. But even the best goalie will falter if his defense cannot keep the puck away for at least a bit of the game, or the offense cannot score.

Aggressiveness in hockey plays a big part in the success of a team. Witness the play of the Broad Street Bullies, the Philadelphia Flyers. They have the best goalie in the business, but most of the other players, except for Bobby Clarke, are pretty mediocre—but they are mean.

An aggressive team will score in spite of itself and will intimidate another even superior skating team. In general, favor a team with the lowest goals against average. This is a good indicator of total team defense. If the goalies are relatively equal, go with the most aggressive team, even if it is not the team with the highest goals-scored average. The reason for this is similar to the reasoning on running-teams in baseball. Always back a team that tries to force mistakes over a team that tends to wait for breaks. If the goalies are equal, a team has to push in order to score more than the other. Bet the pusher. Another major factor is home-court advantage. Some teams rarely lose at home. Keep records on the home and away win-loss records of each team. Do not bet a visiting team if the home team wins a substantial portion of its home games.

In hockey betting, bet the best team unless the odds go above 7-5 against your team. Paying $8 to win $5 is too steep a price. If you bet only the best team, you will expect a certain percentage of winners, but those winners have to pay for your losers. Betting above 7-5 means you have to win two out of three for a profit.

Increase the size of your bets if the team you favor is at even odds or above. This is aimed at taking full advantage of whatever overlays you come across. Decrease your bets in the reverse situation. People have the opposite tendency; they will increase on the lower-odds bets. Yet remember, if you bet on the favorite and lose, you stand to lose more than you would have gained had your team won. The risk is less with the underdog for a greater payoff. If you only bet on the best team, you will probably win at the same or a similar percentage of each type of bet, underdog or favorite. It is better to minimize your potential losses on favorites and maximize your potential winnings on underdogs.

5

The New Games In Town

None of the games discussed in this chapter are new in the strictest sense of the word. Various forms of backgammon have been played since the ancient Egyptians. Modern jai alai was developed in the 1700s. Greyhounds and quarterhorses have been raced since the domestication of each breed. Yet all four games have one thing in common. They are enjoying a tremendous upsurge in popularity and they all owe that increased interest to gambling.

Backgammon sets have become major sellers for toy manufacturers and department stores. Thousands of amateur backgammon players are falling victim to backgammon hustlers—sharpies who know the game requires as much skill as luck and use their knowledge of the odds to relieve naive suckers of excess cash. There are now several hundred professional gamblers who concentrate on backgammon alone to make a more-than-comfortable living.

Dog and quarterhorse racing tracks and jai alai frontons are popping up all over the United States. Jai alai has spread from Florida to Nevada to several points in the Northeast. Parimutuel (state-sanctioned and controlled) quarterhorse racing is now conducted at ninety-four tracks in this country and is also spreading to the population centers of the North and East. Dog racing is now operated at dozens of tracks in ten states. The number of states is expected to double within the next five years.

But the information on how to handicap these sports is largely nonexistent. General gambling books have overlooked all of them. Except for backgammon, they have not been big enough for long enough, to warrant much in the way of complete books or systems to explain how to win. This chapter should remedy this problem by providing betting tips and systems for playing jai alai, dog and quarterhorse races and showing how to play and win at backgammon.

JAI ALAI

Jai alai (pronounced ʼhī-lī) is one of the most exciting gambling games available. It is a fast-paced, handball-like game that uses baskets, called cestas, instead of the hand to propel a hard rubber and goatskin ball against a concrete wall. The ball travels at speeds upward of 150 miles per hour with the players constantly making frantic, yet graceful leaps for the ball.

Jai alai was once called pelota-Basque, or Basque-ball, after the province in Spain where the modern game originated. The words jai alai mean merry festival in Basque; the game was often a highlight of Basque festivals. Most of the players, even in American jai alai, are Basques, imported by American promoters specifically for the purpose of playing the game here. There are now a few American players, but the stars are usually Basque. The American contingent is likely to increase since jai alai is catching on in Florida as an amateur sport.

Most of the jai alai stadiums, called frontons, are in Florida, where the game has been a part of that state's parimutuel setup since the 1930s. However, Nevada also has jai alai and frontons are being built for opening in 1976 in Connecticut and Rhode Island.

The betting at jai alai is similar to horse racing. Bets include win, place, show, quiniela, perfecta, and the double. Games are either two-man-team round robins or singles tournaments. A win bet pays off if the team (or player) wins. A place bet pays off if the team (or individual player) comes in first or second. A show bet pays off if the team or player comes in first, second, or third. These bets are made for $2 or $5 or their multiples. The quiniela ticket costs $2 or $5 and selects two teams (or players) to finish in first and second, in either order. The perfecta costs $3 and selects two teams to come in first and second, in exact order. The $3 double selects the winners by two consecutive races; unlike horse racing, a daily double is not necessarily on the first two matches.

Jai alai is similar to handball but faster and more dangerous. The players are protected only by a helmet and their own quick reflexes from a hard, fast-moving ball, called a pelota. The ball is caught and thrown in one smooth motion by the cesta, a basket-like device connected by strap to the wrist of the jai alai player. The game is played on a three wall court. The object of the game is to throw the pelota against the front wall at such a speed or spin that the opposing player or team cannot return the ball. The ball must be returned either on the fly or in one bounce. The point is lost if the ball is missed or returned out of bounds. On the serve, the ball must bounce back on the return past a white line denoting the serving zone. When a point is decided, the losing team or player returns to the bench and the winner meets the next opponent. The winning team or player continues to play until losing a point; then the new winner holds the court.

Most jai alai games are played with teams—two players to a team, eight teams to a game. To insure full

173

fields, the frontons name official substitutes before the game. In the singles matches, fields are from six to eight players.

In the team game, the teams are listed in jai alai programs in post positions, just as in dog or horse racing, in order to make betting and the parimutuel boards less confusing. Each game starts out with the number one team against the number two team. The winner plays the three team; that winner plays the four team, and so on. The first round ends when all eight teams have had at least one chance to play.

On the first round of play all winning decisions count one point; on the second round, winners receive two points per score. One member of each team plays front court; the other plays back throughout the game. There is no rotation, as in other games, since certain players are experts at either front or back courts. In singles play, the same rules apply, although the players, of course, cover the entire court.

The volleys at jai alai can often become quite spectacular as the players bounce off the side walls, dive off the floor, or carom off the screen separating the fans from the action. The trick in winning is to throw the ball against the front wall so that your opponent has a tough time returning it.

According to the rules of the game, as played in the United States, if a player fails to try to return even an impossible shot, he faces suspension, fines, and possible banishment for life from the profession. So there is little dogging it; no matter which team or player you bet on, at least you get your money's worth. Jai alai is alone among American sports in that it has never been hit by so much as a hint of scandal. It is hard for a player to throw a game if he is going to get kicked out just for not trying. Also, he faces banishment or fines if he talks to or signals anyone (even a simple wave to a friend) in the audience anytime after entering the players' room before the start of the day's action. In some frontons the players not on the court reside in a cage kept away from the audience in order to further reduce temptations of fraternizing with the fans. Further isolation is provided by the language and ethnic barriers between fans and players. Most players are Basques; they rarely stay in the United States after the jai alai seasons—or their careers—have ended.

Fixing is unlikely in jai alai, but it is not impossible. Since most of the players are from the not-terribly-rich province of Spain, they are not paid outrageous sums of money like American athletes. The players at the Miami fronton once tried to strike for higher wages, but the fronton operators just imported a new load of Basques and killed the strike. So those seemingly extreme measures may be necessary to prevent dishonesty. Any time an athlete stands to make more money by losing than by winning, there will always be a temptation to cheat.

But in jai alai betting it is not the fixes you have to worry about, it is how to handicap. The major problem in handicapping is that the teams change from game to game. The fronton's equivalent to a racing secretary puts together perhaps ten team matches for the night. In match three, for instance, Randy and Alberto will be teammates, and in game four each will be playing with different partners. (All jai alai players, by the way, are referred to by their first names only in the program—Basque tradition.) How Randy will play with Alberto or with another jai alai player cannot be determined by the program. The frontons do not publish statistics on individual teams, only on the past performances of the players in particular games. Randy's entry in match three, for instance, will include his win-place-show total for the times he has played in the third game of each meeting of the year. It will not include his record as Alberto's partner. This makes about as much sense as recording a jockey's win percentage by race—the number of the race or match has no bearing on the outcome. The only effect on the outcome is Randy's overall win percentage and his ability to play with Alberto.

So if you are going to bet on jai alai, you will have to keep records on the performances of each team. Most players are either front or back court specialists. The best front court player can lose consistently if the man playing back court keeps fouling him up. Likewise, an average player can be saved repeatedly by a brilliant player. Two great jai alai players may be heavily bet everytime they are together; but in reality your records may show that they spend much of the game competing with each other, grandstanding, or sulking. As any follower of professional sports knows, great athletes often have massive egos that can flare up at the most inappropriate moments. It is up to you to record the idiosyncracies of the jai alai players as they are matched with equal, weaker, or stronger partners.

If you are not willing to keep team records, then only bet the singles games. There are usually two of these a night, and there are overall win records available for these players. Bet the player with the best win percentage, unless he is in a losing streak. Another suggestion for singles play is to keep weekly records on the best singles players. The player with the best overall win record will be bet heavily; the player on a winning streak may be ignored.

There is no substitute for keeping your own records in jai alai. The program information is simply inadequate and will only lead you to playing favorites. Because of the state and fronton tax bite, playing favorites will result in an overall loss.

Most jai alai bettors are casual players who are just out for fun for an afternoon or evening. They are willing to pay for the fun, but not willing to learn how to win. So, it is not that difficult for an informed bettor to consistently beat the public choice.

Play the team with the best win percentage for playing together. Ignore overall win records for games not with the partner for that particular game. Bet win and place for singles play and team play. The best team or player does not always win. A lucky shot can cost you a game, but the consistent team or player should at least come in second. Do not play any team or player if the odds go below 2-1. You are not going to win all the time; it is better to assure a reasonable profit for the times you finish out of the money.

In a perfecta bet if you think number two is the best team and number four is the second best, for $3 you bet the two-four perfecta. If the result of the match is exactly team two first and team four in second place, you win the perfecta. If four comes in first you lose, so it is wise to reverse the bet for an additional $3; for $6 you have both teams in either order.

For a $2 investment on the quiniela you get the same thing—two teams in either order—and the payoffs on the perfecta are not usually three times that of the quiniela. So the quiniela bet is recommended, but only if two contenders have a decided edge over the rest of the field and they are not in adjacent or nearly adjacent post positions. For instance, never bet a one-two quiniela or perfecta; it is almost impossible to win.

Consider that in the first game of the match, team one plays team two and the loser is eliminated from the round. The winning team keeps playing until it loses a point. The loser does not get back into the game until the end of the first round. By that time, two or three of the teams will have several points, and one of your teams will be lagging far behind and will have to win at least twice the second

177

round to stay even. Or if you bet the four-five quiniela, number four has a chance for only one point in the first round before facing number five. The situation you are facing is that one of your teams is always in the position of keeping the other out of the money. A team that gets one or less points in the first round is greatly hampered, and its odds of winning or placing are significantly reduced.

Do not bet the quiniela unless the two best contenders are separated by three or more post positions, e.g., team three and team six.

As for doubles, if you have a definite choice in two consecutive matches, bet the double. Or if you have narrowed it down to a ceiling of two contenders in each match, bet all possible combinations. If the number of contenders in both matches exceeds four, do not bet the double; your investment is too steep for your chances of hitting.

GREYHOUND RACING

Greyhound racing has had a shady history in the United States. In the early days of the sport, crowds were appalled by the finishes of each race. Rabbits were used to lure the dogs to run and when the dogs finally caught the live jackrabbit, they ripped the screaming animal apart in full view of the squeamish bettors. This somewhat limited greyhound racing as a spectator sport.

Then the mechanical rabbit was invented; the dogs would chase it just as well without offering the public that gory climax. But the first promoters to see the possibilities in greyhound racing as a mass audience sport happened to be Mobsters. Al Capone was a big wheel in the early days as a partial owner of the major dog track in Hialeah, Florida; other gangsters were involved in other tracks.

These gangsters were rarely satisfied with just skimming money off the top—taxing the bets, charging admission, etc. They also fixed races by drugging dogs, overfeeding, overwatering or overworking them just before races—even sanding an animal's feet—anything to eliminate contenders and set the race up for one dog. Scandals hit the greyhound industry and the sport is still less than trusted by the wary gambler.

But from all outward appearances the sport is honest today. It is still not humane, however. The mechanical rabbit only prevents the public destruction of rabbits. The dogs are still trained on live, warm jackrabbits. To get the taste of blood, training sometimes involves tying down the rabbit, while the dog runs at it and tears it apart. Some more humane trainers find it unnecessary to use live rabbits, but the great majority of greyhound trainers are not a particularly enlightened bunch.

Humane considerations aside, however, it is possible to win at dog racing. There are two basic advantages that dog racing has over both thoroughbred and harness racing.

1.   There are a limited number of factors that will determine the outcome of the race.
2.   There is no jockey or driver to blow or throw the race.

Dog racing is now certifiably honest. There is no opportunity left to overfeed or drug dogs. On racing days the dogs are brought to the equivalent of receiving barns, hours before racing, thus preventing any betting interests from interfering with the animals. Drug tests are required and security is stiff. This does not preclude trainers from undertraining or overtraining a dog in order to throw a race, however. But the widespread practice of eliminating several contenders in any race is a thing of the past. It is just too hard to do anymore. In the various forms of horse racing, the easiest way to fix a race is through the driver or jockey. The dog is on his own once the race begins and cannot be affected by the betting proclivities of his handlers. It is immaterial to the dog how much money he stands to win in a race—he just wants to get that rabbit.

A standard dog race is with six to nine dogs at 5/16 or 3/8 of a mile around an oval track. Betting at the dogs is modeled after horse racing. It offers win, place, and show bets; the daily double; quinielas; and sometimes exactas. A win ticket pays off if the dog wins; a place ticket pays if the dog comes in first or second; a show ticket pays if the animal runs first, second, or third. So do not throw away those place tickets if your dog runs first instead of second; the ticket is still good. The daily double wins if you select the winner of two successive races, usually the first two of the day. A quiniela is selecting the first two finishers in a race, in either order. In an exacta you select the first two finishers in a race in exact order.

How to Beat the Dogs

Each dog has its own individual running style. Some are quick starters, others lag behind. Some like to run on the outside part of the track; others on the inside. Some always take the turns sharply; others go way wide every time. Some dogs try to fight with others about to pass them. What occurs in any typical race is bedlam. Wide-running dogs slam into dogs veering inside; both cut off straight runners. Several dogs are eliminated at the first turn by all the bumping. So the best dog does not necessarily win. But what makes it easier for the handicapper is that dogs retain these running habits in almost all their races. If you know how each dog will react once the race begins, you can predict the outcome of a race.

Class is another major factor with dogs. Final speed is a difficult way to gauge an animal's ability—unless you keep charts of average times run each day, which is certainly too much for the average bettor. The track will change from day to day, causing variations in final times for dogs of equal class. To determine greater relative speed, get an average final time for each dog. The track variances should average out. If one dog has a decided edge in speed, it may be worthy of a bet. But class is a better determinant.

There are five grades in greyhound racing—A, B, C, D, and E. After a win in one grade, the dog moves up to the next class. The dog moves down after three finishes out of the money in one class, providing he is in condition. Dogs usually stay in condition; traffic problems or better dogs primarily cause losses.

It is necessary to keep records on the running habits of each dog at the track you attend. There is little substitute for knowing the animals. A good memory helps, but a notebook is easier just to record running styles. Fast-breaking dogs will have an advantage over late-running dogs; they get into less trouble going into the turn and since there is no pace involved, do not worry about the dog running out of gas.

Post position in a particular race is a final determinant—where each dog is in relation to his opponents and their running habits. For example, a six-dog race in which the class is class B and the race at 5/16 of a mile. Following is a capsule description of each dog. Numbers refer to their post positions in this race.

Number one: Has early speed; tends to bear out badly on the turns and runs a bit wide on the straightaways. Won its last race from the outside post.

Number two: Slow starter, out of the money in last two races. Runs straight.

Number three: Fast starter but veers to rail immediately after break, takes turns sharply. Was second the last time out in same class when in post position two.

Number four: Fast starter, straight runner, eliminated at turn in last two races in class B.

Number five: Come-from-behind dog, bears out slightly on turns; has lost last three races.

Number six: Average starter, straight runner, won last on outside post when other dogs got into bumping match.

What is likely to happen? The number one and number three dogs will slam into each other or the number two dog. All three will probably be eliminated on the turn. Number two does not move fast enough in the early stages to avoid being cut off. Number four will have a straight course for a change and has an advantage over the slow-starting number five. Number six is disadvantaged by his class; he won the last race by default. But the three outside dogs are the contenders.

In dog racing because of the rough running, it is often recommended that you not bet a dog to win, but instead bet several in a quiniela box. (Though in the case cited, the number four dog would seem to have the race locked up and should be bet to win and place.) For example, if you have decided that dogs one, two, and three will be eliminated in the running, boxing the remaining three dogs will cost $6—$2 each for the four-five, five-six, and four-six combinations. If one of the dogs gets knocked out, gets a bad start, or just does not run his race, you are still in business.

This is a recommended bet in greyhound racing. The payoffs are better than for straight win, yet the risk is somewhat diminished.

For those who do not have the time to keep records or are merely casual followers of dog racing, try this formula for beating the dogs. Take the two dogs with the best early speed and box with the classiest dog. This information will appear in even the most primitive of dog racing programs. The classiest dog will be the one who has raced successfully and consistently in the highest class and/or has won the most money per starts. Again this box will cost $6. The advantages here are that one of those speed dogs will be likely to finish either first or second. And the best dog should be able to get up for second even with traffic problems. This will not always occur, but the probable payoff justifies the bet. You are playing with the percentages and a profit is inevitable.

QUARTERHORSE RACING

The quarterhorse is a peculiarly American animal of bastard ancestry, bred for quick starts and stops, for running up and down rough terrain, and for general stamina. In a race, his best distance is under a quarter mile; beyond that, his speed is much slower than the average thoroughbred. But unlike the thoroughbred his legs are not spindly and do not break as easily. The thoroughbred has been inbred over centuries to increase the breed's speed; this has resulted in faster, but less sound horses. The quarterhorse is significantly sounder, but will lose any race with a thoroughbred at a quarter mile or more.

Cowboys consider a quarterhorse underdeveloped and unready for serious work until it hits the age of five years, but the horses begin racing at two years old, just like thoroughbred or trotting horses.

In 1975 there were ninety-four tracks in the United States conducting parimutuel quarterhorse racing. Some of these tracks also conduct thoroughbred racing; often both types are run on the same day. Probably the most famous quarterhorse track in the United States is Ruidoso Downs in New Mexico. The track also runs a cheap thoroughbred meeting, but it is best known for conducting the annual All-American Futurity, the third jewel in quarterhorse racing's triple crown and the richest horse race in North America. The race has a gross purse close to $1,000,000. About forty-five to fifty additional tracks hold nonparimutuel quarterhorse racing—mostly county fairs where the betting is informal between spectators and participants. Quarterhorse racing also occurs anywhere some rancher or farmer has a quarter-mile straightaway and a neighbor with a horse to challenge his own.

On the bush circuit—those nonparimutuel places particularly—the racing can get pretty wild. For one thing, the horses do not always have jockeys, at least not jockeys in the standard sense. One of the top women jockeys in the United States, Mary Bacon, got her start at these bush tracks. Bacon recently described one race in which she was the only human jockey. One horse was ridden by a chicken, the other had a string of tin cans tied to its back—just so the horse would think there was some reason to keep running once the race was started. (Don't ever let anyone tell you horses are intelligent.) By the end of the race, the horse dragging the tin cans had fallen behind, but as Bacon explained, "I got beat by the chicken."

Providing the horses have human jockeys, quarterhorse racing can be one of the easier sports to beat. Quarterhorses are sound and consistent. And there are few factors to consider when handicapping the races. The factors to consider are: speed, tendency to bear in or out at the start, starting ability, distance, and track condition. And that is it.

Quarterhorse races are run at distances of 250 yards to 440 yards on straightaways. No turns means that there is no advantage to particular post positions, but the handicapper should keep a record of horses that tend to bear in or out at the start. These horses often bump or cut off opponents, eliminating themselves and the horse bumped. If the best horse in the race is caught between a horse that has a habit of veering left and one that veers right, his chances are significantly reduced.

The short distance eliminates any problems about pace. The horses just get out there and run. At 250 yards a horse does not tire; he loses because the other horse is simply faster at the distance. The short distances also make it imperative that the horse get a good start. A standard 440-yard race may take twenty-two to twenty-four seconds. A 250-yard race will take much less. A 1/5-second delay at the start will cause the horse to lose one length. There is not enough time in the race to make up that length, so the jockey must be able to break the horse well. Watch the riders before even making your first bet; eliminate those jockeys who consistently start poorly. They may win occasionally, but the odds are too much against it.

If a horse consistently breaks too slowly at the 250-yard distance, he may be able to hit stride better in the 440-yard race. But it is a good idea to wait until the horse has one such race under his belt before betting. A good start at the quarter mile distance is just as necessary. The other distances sanctioned by the U.S. Quarterhorse Association are 300, 350, and 400 yards. Some tracks are beginning to run longer races up to 700 yards because the public tends to get tired of watching races that are over in the time it takes to sneeze. With these races, since the horses will have to go around a turn, watch out for sharp-starting horses on the inside. Late-starting horses should be on the outside to have any kind of chance; otherwise they will be blocked.

The main factor to pay attention to, however, is speed. How fast does the horse usually run at this distance? If a horse has run consistently faster than the others in the race, he will win. Make sure, however, that the condition of the track is suited to this particular horse. His top speeds may be accomplished on fast tracks. Avoid him on sloppy or slow-going tracks if his record shows no races on off-tracks or poor ability to handle such tracks.

Since the factors are obvious and limited, quarterhorse racing is easier to predict than other forms of racing. As proof of that, up to 50 percent of the favorites win compared to 30 to 35 percent in thoroughbred racing. This is one sport in which if you blindly bet the favorite to win each race, you should come up with a profit.

Any betting game that can be reduced to such a limited number of factors is ready-made for the casual gambler. Unfortunately quarterhorse racing is concentrated away from the major centers of population; access is limited primarily to those in the South and West. But Northerners can take heart. A major quarterhorse track is under construction near New York City and groups in several metropolitan areas are pushing for its establishment closer to urban America.

BACKGAMMON

Backgammon is the "in" game among gambling hustlers today. An operator of a private backgammon club recently estimated at least 150 gamblers in the United States alone now earn over $150,000 per year hustling backgammon. They are aided in their quest to fleece suckers by the general impression held by nearly everyone

that backgammon is a game of chance. It is not. It involves as much skill as poker or handicapping races and
sports events. There comes a time in each backgammon
game when the player has to make a decision on moving
his pieces one way or another. How each player reacts to
these decision-making situations will determine whether
he usually wins or usually loses. Move one way, and the
odds are with you; move another, and you will probably
lose.

Backgammon is an ancient game enjoying new-found
popularity. Modern backgammon strongly resembles the
children's games of Parcheesi and Sorry. Each player has
a home base to which he tries to bring all his pieces; a
wrong move and the opponent can send a piece back to
square one. For those unfamiliar with the play of
backgammon, the rules follow. An illustration of the
backgammon board and the opening position is on page
190.

The backgammon board is split into four rectangles or
tables. Each of these tables, as you can see in the illustration, contains six triangles, called points. One player has
the twelve points on one side of the board; the other
player has the other twelve points on the opposite side. In
the illustration, the white side is closest to the bottom. The
six points on the right are part of white's inner table. The
six points on the left are the outer table. The two tables
are separated by a bar. Likewise, black's inner table is to
white's right; the outer table is diagonal to white's inner
table.

In the opening position, white's men or pieces are at
varying distances from his inner table. The object is to
move his pieces in this direction: from opponent's inner
table to opponent's outer table to white outer table to

white inner table and then off the board. Black also moves in this manner; thus, the opposing pieces move in opposite directions.

The pieces move according to the numbers showing on the throw of a pair of dice. A piece moves along the points; up to five pieces can fit on a point at one time. The high roll moves first. The two dice-units thrown can be used separately or combined. Thus, if the throw is seven—a three on one die, a four on another—one piece can be moved seven points or the seven can be split with one man moving four and another three. The split must exactly coincide with the roll. (A seven roll on a three-four combination does not allow one piece to move five, the other two.) When doubles are thrown, the total move is doubled. Two fours, for instance, allows a total move of sixteen points; four men move four points or two men move eight, or any other combination.

When an opponent has two or more men on a point, his opponent cannot rest on that point, though he may go on to the point following if his move can carry him that far. If a single piece sits on a point, this is called a "blot" and is a vulnerable position. If the opponent lands a man on this point (only on an exact number), the piece is removed from the table, placed on the bar, and must be brought back to the opponent's inner table, ready for the long journey all around the board. Until this blotted piece returns, the player cannot move any other men, and the piece can only be brought back on a point on the opponent's inner table that is not already held. This means that a player could lose several turns trying to bring back the blotted piece. Also, if the player has begun bearing pieces off the board and another piece gets blotted, he is prevented from bearing off any other pieces until that blotted piece gets back to his inner table.

The first player to get all his pieces borne off wins.

He wins double or gammon if the opponent has not been able to bear off a single piece. He wins triple if the opponent has one or more pieces on the bar—blotted out and waiting to re-enter the game—or in the winner's inner table. This is called backgammon and pays off at triple the agreed-upon bet.

Hustlers take advantage of an option in backgammon called doubling. At anytime during the game, either player can offer to double the stake. If the offer is refused, the player who initiated the offer automatically wins. The option is what defeats most amateurs. It is hard to turn down because you immediately lose if you do. If you accept, the chances are you will lose anyway. The game may seem even, but your opponent would not have offered to double unless he was fairly sure of winning. What is the best strategy in this case? If your opponent has no pieces in your inner table, but you do have one or more in his, you are in a vulnerable situation. If you also are in danger of one or more blots, decline the opportunity to double. If, however, the game seems even, go ahead and double. But, this presupposes that you will pay attention to the following advice on how to play winning backgammon.

The worst possible move any player can make is to leave a piece unprotected; a blot leads to all sorts of calamities. Try, at all times, to avoid a blot situation. Take those two lone whites in black's inner table on the illustration of the opening position. Always move them together on doubles. All the black pieces are going through there, making them particularly vulnerable. Do not ever separate them. Never break off one man unless it not only leaves a safe point, but it can also get to a safe point on that move. (A safe point is one in which two or more pieces are resting.) Never permit a blot to occur, except in your own inner table when all your opponent's pieces have been removed from there. The only situation in which you would break off a piece is to hit an opponent's blot and force him off the table. However, try to do this only when your opponent's pieces are in front of you. For instance, if all of black's remaining pieces were moving from your outer table to his outer table, and you are close to your inner table and black cannot move backwards to hit your blot, you are invulnerable. Break off and hit, but move to a safe spot as soon as possible. Generally, however, try to hit your opponent's blot with two men.

This is the major point of strategy involved in simple winning backgammon—never expose your pieces unnecessarily. Volumes have been written on backgammon strategy but the easiest way to win is to avoid losing. You may not always win this way, but leaving yourself open with a blot generally means you will lose. As for doubling, offer a double yourself if one or more of your opponent's pieces is exposed or has already been knocked off the board. Any player who allows himself to fall into blots will usually lose. Take advantage of it. Otherwise, always play cautiously and quit if you start losing regularly, particularly to strangers. A lot of hustlers use loaded dice; others may be honest but far more skilled. Do not multiply your losses; quit while you are behind.

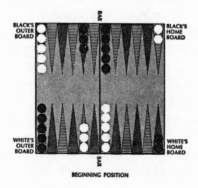

BEGINNING POSITION

6

Elections

Betting on elections is a fine old American tradition. Bets have ranged from the $500,000 high-roller Arnold Rothstein wagered on Herbert Hoover's chances in 1928 to Edward Payson Weston's promise to walk all the way from Boston to Washington in ten days if Abe Lincoln won the 1860 election. (Weston paid off, but Rothstein was murdered just before Hoover won, thus canceling the bet.)

Most election betting is on the presidential contests with lesser action for the lesser offices. Bettors generally bet their biases or hopes with little attention to the actual chances of a candidate. Yet the outcome of a presidential election is the most predictable of bets. Year after year, the same voting patterns prevail; the same issues cause voters to switch or stay with a political party.

With this in mind, this author has developed a formula for handicapping presidential elections. Barring any unforeseen switches in American voting patterns, such as that which occurred during the Depression, this formula can be used successfully for years to come to determine, months ahead of time and often before either of the major parties has selected its candidate, the probable winner of the next presidential contest. The formula described would have correctly predicted the outcome of every presidential election since 1932. (Elections prior to 1932 were determined by different voter-identification patterns and issue-party connections.) This formula predicts that the Democrats, regardless of which candidate they select, will win the 1976 election, unless economic conditions drastically improve or the United States gets into another war. A chart of this formula follows.

PRESIDENTIAL ELECTIONS PREDICTION CHART

	Democrats	Republicans	Either party
Base figure	43	29	
Candidate is incumbent			+20
Party in power 8 years or more			−5
Party spending most money			+5
Country in all-out war			+10 incumbent party
Major scandal involving candidate			−5
U.S. in limited war		+10	
Major issues discussed:			
foreign policy	−10	+10	
domestic issues	+10	−10	
In recession	+10		
In depression	+20		
Ethnic presidential candidate	+20	+10	
Ethnic Veep candidate	+10	+5	
Major party walkout or third-party candidate			−10 to original party of third = 1 party candidate

The base figure for each party represents the percentage of American voters who identify themselves in polls as either strong or weak Republicans or Democrats. The Democrats have been the majority party in this country since the upheaval of the Great Depression in the 1930s. In any given year, at least 43 percent of all Americans will identify themselves as Democrats. In 1964 that figure rose to 49 percent, sunk in the following nine years, then rose again. But for the purposes of this chart, use the rock bottom figure of 43 percent. The Republican party claims the allegiance of at least 29 percent of the voters.

It is immediately obvious that the Democrats have a great advantage going into any national election. All else being equal, the Democrats would win every presidential election. But things are rarely equal around election time and there are certain issues and events that can cause major shifts in the remaining 28 percent of the voters, and indeed can affect large numbers of those persons who describe themselves as weak Democrats or Republicans. These factors are enumerated in the chart and point totals are assigned to them according to the number of voters likely to be swayed from or to a particular party or candidate.

It must be stressed that not all voters will react in the ways described herein, but the average voter, not the party regular or the particularly educated voter, will determine elections.

While several factors can cause a voter to switch his party allegiance or decide to vote for one party over another, the major causes of voters' shifts can be summed up in two words: recession and war. It may be a cliche to call the Democrats the party of war and the Republicans the party of recession, but that's the way the American voter perceives each party. Ever since the Depression, the

Republicans have been associated in the American mind with economic troubles; whenever there is a recession their chances will plummet. The Democrats, ever since Korea, have been associated with war—not all-out war like World Wear II—but the nationally frustrating, no-win, seemingly interminable kind like the Korean and Vietnam wars.

Both recession and limited war will cause deep-seated insecurity for the American voter. With recession, of course, there is the ever-present personal fear of losing a job or otherwise getting into a financial bind. Families and the elderly fear being wiped out; young people are unemployed at alarming rates; millions are underemployed, stuck in jobs they hate because that is all that is available; women, older workers, and minorities are in particularly precarious positions during hard times. This all leads to financial uneasiness and voters' long memories link this insecurity with the party of Herbert Hoover.

With limited war, there is the personal fear of involvement and worry over the great financial and physical cost of the war. But primarily the war becomes internalized as a source of national failure and frustration. The country's inability to win a war becomes a threat to the individual voter's security as an American. That is why in periods of limited war there is such an increase in visible patriotism: Red scares, flag decals, etc.

This theory also explains the resurgence of the Republican party in times of international crises. The American voters seem to feel that the Republican party's conservative, patriotic response to the situation will alleviate the world's, and their own, doubts about the power of the United States. The average voter identifies with the United States as a world power; in terms of limited war, this identification is threatened by minor powers, and the Republican party feeds this patriotic need.

This attitude also prevails in certain other periods of international crises, but it is intensified during limited war. Again, the crisis cannot be cut and dried but has to be a frustrating diplomatic or military defeat, such as when the United States "lost" China. For the purposes of predicting elections, however, the Republicans will only benefit in an election if the overwhelming and obvious concern of the majority of voters is international affairs.

Just as in times of economic crises, the Democrats feed the psychic needs of the voter who is worried about his or her individual place in society—employment, financial security, possessions. People who lose jobs or are worried about losing them do not need pronouncements that the recession is about to "bottom out" or that the country can stand a few million unemployed. Whether true or not, the voters will respond to the Democrats who stress their "rights" to full employment and financial security. Whether a recession is present or not, the Democrats will benefit if the major concern of the voters is in domestic areas. Again, if international threats are not present, the voter turns to domestic concerns and his normal preference for the Democratic party will prevail.

This favoring of the Republicans in times of international crises does not apply if the crisis is an all-out war. The all-out war causes a different reaction by citizens. There is a pulling together, a feeling of camaraderie, all intensified by the national will to win and the overwhelming agreement that the country is in the right. This reaction will cause voters to back the incumbent party even more that in normal times. Disillusionment about war will set in only when it is clear, through design or simple failure, that victory cannot be gained militarily. It is an interesting point that while the Republicans won in 1952 and 1968 with a promise to end the war, they did not end the Korean and Vietnam military actions through a victory.

Yet the issue was sufficiently defused by claiming partial victory and ending major United States involvement amid a good deal of saber rattling.

What if neither of these situations is present, or one or both are present but only to limited degrees? Then other factors may decide the election. These factors include incumbency, corruption, money spent during elections, party dissension, ethnicity, and voters' feeling that it is "time for a change."

In this century, an incumbent president has been defeated only twice. Taft in 1912 because of a major split in his party and Hoover in 1932 because of the Depression. Voters, unless they perceive a major reason to change administrations, will not throw out an incumbent president. Part of the reason for this is the tremendous good will that the American public has toward its president. Even after Richard Nixon resigned in disgrace following the Watergate scandals, he still placed high in the annual most-admired men poll of United States citizens.

Another reason is that everybody knows who the president is and the opposition candidate will have to spend much of his pre-election campaign getting his name known to the American public. By virtue of his office, anything the president does is news and is reported thoroughly by the news media. So the president starts off with a higher percentage of voters who recognize his name and he will always receive more publicity than the challenger. This name-recognition factor alone will give him hundreds of thousands of votes. The third reason is that the typical American voter is basically conservative and will not lightly boot a chief of state out of office.

One way an incumbent can lose is by a major split in his party. As mentioned before, the split in the Republican party in 1912 led to the first Democratic party victory in twenty years. The third-party candidacy of George

Wallace contributed greatly to the defeat of Hubert Humphrey in 1968. Yet two segments of the Democratic party split off in 1948 and Harry Truman still won. Why did Truman win and Humphrey lose? Truman won because as far as most voters were concerned, there was no deep-rooted reason to shift parties. Humphrey lost because the voters were shifting away from the Democrats in 1968 because of the war. Again, the American voter is conservative; he generally believes in the two-party system. Something drastic has to wrench him out of that mold. It did not happen in 1948 and the two splinter groups shared that small minority of voters who were dissatisfied with the major parties.

George Wallace was the recipient of millions of votes by people who might have stayed home, voted Republican, or reluctantly voted for the Democrat. The 1968 election was extremely close and it is difficult to determine what might have happened had Wallace not run. But it is clear that Wallace did run because of his and his supporters' disaffection from the Democratic party, and the people who voted for him were specifically voting against the Democratic party. Voter trends will determine whether a third party candidacy has an effect on an election. If, for instance, the country is in the middle of a recession and a Democratic faction breaks off and runs on a third-party line, it is unlikely that it will have a significant effect on the voters. The pattern of voting Democratic in the times of economic crises is too set. The time for third-party, Democratic offshoots is when Republicans are in the ascendancy.

Mere dissension within the party ranks will not lose an election, nor will nomination of a candidate seemingly in the extremist wing of that party. Instead, an extremist may be nominated by the party when the voter trends indicate that the party has little or no chance of winning, thus creating a vacuum in the nominating process. A case in point was the Goldwater debacle of 1964. Except for last-minute abortive candidacies by two or three Republican governors, Barry Goldwater was the only Republican actively seeking the nomination for 1964. His backers were the only people working and spending money to get that nomination. At that time close to 50 percent of all voters considered themselves Democrats; Lyndon Johnson was immensely popular; Vietnam was in the future. The Republicans had no chance of winning, so Goldwater received the nomination almost by default. The Republicans, however, did not lose because of Goldwater; they nominated Goldwater because they were going to lose. Many less conservative Republicans did not back the candidate, but the nonsupport had no meaning; the Republicans were going to lose anyway.

Likewise, if a party is in the ascendancy, no amount of dissension can cut it down. In 1960, for example, there were great rifts in the Democratic Party. Johnson and Kennedy factions hated each other; Stevenson and Kennedy factions were equally spiteful. Nobody, in fact, was too crazy about anybody else. But the party smelled victory. A recession had occurred during Eisenhower's last term. It had been six years since the end of the Korean War. So dissension played a small part in the election and Kennedy won even though he was a virtual unknown next to his opponent, Nixon.

Dissension within party ranks can only defeat a party already in trouble; nomination of an extremist as the party candidate is usually an indicator that the party bosses and likely candidates expect defeat. Third-party efforts generally occur only when there is a great turning away from the more central principles of one of the major parties. Party members, in general, however, will not be dissatisfied with party policies when the issues favor their party ideology.

The pull of war and economics on the American voter is so great that national corruption and scandal have little or no bearing on the presidential vote. The Watergate scandal broke before the 1972 election but was pretty much disregarded by the voter because it did not seem to have too much to do with him. The voter was pretty satisfied with Nixon; he thought Nixon would end the war soon and keep the national head up high in terms of world opinion. Economic conditions were okay, so why change?

Likewise, in 1964 Lyndon Johnson was involved in the Bobby Baker scandal in which his top aides were going to jail for selling favors, etc. Yet few voters considered the scandal important. In fact, no major scandal involving a president or his administration has ever resulted in his or his party's defeat in a presidential election. Voters just do not think that way. (This is not true, however, in local elections. Corruption closer to home is dealt with more directly by voters.) If something else accompanies the scandal, such as war or recession, then there is a change in votes, but not a scandal itself. The two most corrupt administrations in the past two hundred years have been those of U. S. Grant and Warren Harding. No voter switches followed those scandals.

However, there is a slight drop-off in votes of a party that has been in office eight years or more. The voter will get tired of one party and start expressing feelings that "it's time for a change." This is a slight factor, however, unless accompanied with other reasons for voter shifts.

The money spent during an election campaign also has a small effect. Certain voters are swayed by television commercials and the number of times each day they see the name of a candidate. For a challenger, publicity is particularly essential to be in the race at all. If the voter does not know the name of a candidate, how can he be expected to vote for him? So there can be a bit of an edge in recognizability if one party spends more money than the other.

Finally, the ethnic background of a candidate can have a significant effect on his chances. Most candidates have been and probably will be in the future Protestants, mostly of British extraction. In some ways this country is still run by a Prostestant elite, or at least it is perceived that way by millions of voters of varying ethnic backgrounds—Irish Catholics, blacks, Jews, Italians, Poles, etc. When someone who is not Protestant is nominated as president or vice-president, millions of voters who are aware of the traditional ethnic background of the presidency will vote for the ethnic candidate. This effect will be more pronounced if the candidate is Democratic because the normal preference of these voters is generally Democratic. But there will even be a shift toward the Republicans. The importance of this shift is not so much in numbers, however, but in where these voters are. People who vote this way are big-city voters in states with high electoral votes. A major shift in their voting can win a close election. Even if the candidate does not win the overall popular vote, he will still take the electoral vote and that is what counts, which is what happened in 1960. John Kennedy did not win because he looked better than Richard Nixon on television, though that helped. He won because a significant number of ethnic voters were concerned that "one of us" be elected over "one of them."

You may have noticed that there is no provision in the chart for charisma, personality, or any of those other popular qualities attributed to presidential candidates. There is a reason for that. The contention by voters that they vote the man, not the party is erroneous. They vote out of fear; if there are no prevalent fears, they will go with the incumbent or the Democrat; their natural conservatism will prevail. Charisma may have a bearing on which candidate a party chooses, but once the general election is on, the candidates are so packaged, nothing but image is left.

There is a famous oddsmaker in Las Vegas who claims he made a bundle off the 1948 election by betting Truman because an informal poll of his indicated that women would not vote for a man with a mustache, meaning Thomas Dewey. This is nonsense. Dewey may have been stiff and formal; he may have looked, as one pundit claimed, like the little man on top of a wedding cake; but this had little to do with people's failure to vote for him. He lost because there was no reason to throw out the incumbent, nothing that the voter was worried about that a vote for Dewey would help. In the Eisenhower elections, Eisenhower's margin was aided by the fact he was a war hero, but he would have won anyway. (Is there anyone who will claim that Richard Nixon ever won an election on personality?)

Specific issues like inflation come under domestic concerns and are not considered an important issue alone, in terms of the national vote. If people have money, they do not care about the cost of living—at least not enough to change their vote. It is when the source of money is threatened that the vote is affected.

Following is a workout of the results of the 1968, 1960, 1948, and 1936 elections. The first three were close, the latter was not; all four have the common quality, however, that at least one source predicted the election would be won by the eventual loser.

1936

Roosevelt

		Landon	
43	base figure	29	base figure
+20	incumbent	+5	most money spent
+10	major issues domestic	−10	
+20	in depression		
73	Total	24	Total

1948

Truman

		Dewey	
43	base figure	29	base figure
+20	incumbent	+5	most money spent
−5	party in power		
−10	party splits		
48	Total	34	Total

1960

Kennedy

		Nixon	
43	base figure	29	base figure
20	ethnic candidate	−5	in power 8 years
		+5	money spent
63	Total	29	Total

1968

Humphrey

		Nixon	
43	base figure	29	base figure
−5	in power 8 years	+5	most money spent in
−10	major issues intern'l.	+10	limited war
+10	ethnic veep candidate	+10	
−10	major party split	+5	
28	Total	58	Total

In 1936, Roosevelt won because he was an incumbent Democrat during a Depression. *Literary Digest*, of course, predicted Alf Landon as the victor, but there was still far too much ill feeling about the Republican role in the Depression for Landon to win anything other than the states of Maine and Vermont.

In 1948, Truman won as the incumbent in a year when while there was a party split, no one issue overwhelmed the campaign. There was no reason for the voters to change parties.

In 1960, Kennedy won for three reasons. One, there are more Democrats than Republicans. Two, the Republicans had been in office for eight years. And three, his Irish-Catholic heritage enabled him to take the electoral votes of most of the larger states with big-city ethnic majorities. Notice that no points were given in these two elections for the types of issues voters were most concerned about. No points should be given unless the difference is very obvious, such as during the 1968 election with the Vietnam War or 1952 with the Korean War. Also remember that just because a candidate keeps hammering on one point, it does not necessarily mean the voters are concerned over it. Rely on public opinion polls and not politicians for these indications. For example, with all the coverage given the Red scare and domestic communism in 1952, it may be assumed that voters cast the Democrats out of office in that year for reasons other than Korea and foreign policy. But in polls conducted at the time, few voters considered it a major issue or, in fact, an issue at all.

In 1968 Nixon won because of the Vietnam War and because there was a major split in the Democratic party. If George Wallace had not run on a third-party ticket, it is still unlikely that Humphrey would have won because those disaffected Democrats were just as likely to vote for

Nixon as Humphrey, and if loathe to do that, they probably would have just stayed home.

Thus we come to 1976. Which party is likely to win? From the use of this formula it would appear that the Democrats are a cinch. Everything is going for them. The Democrats should be able to overcome the bias in favor of incumbents. Ford will be the first incumbent to lose an election since Herbert Hoover in 1932. Here's the chart for the 1976 election.

Democrats		*Republicans*	
43	base figure	29	base figure
		+20	incumbent
		−5	in power 8 years
		+5	most money spent
+10	domestic issues	−10	
+10	recession		
63	Total	39	Total

This, of course, assumes that the current recession will last until election day—not exactly a rash assumption. It also assumes that the United States will not get into a prolonged war before then. (Quick actions like the Mayaguez do not count; they do not last long enough for the voter patterns to be affected. One month before the election, ask ten people at random what Mayaguez means to them and eight out of ten will likely say it is the name of a song usually played as a solo on a Spanish guitar.)

If there is an ethnic presidential or vice-presidential candidate on the Democratic ticket, the electoral vote, at least, will be larger. Ford's only chance to win is by ending the recession immediately and trying to force the American public back into an overwhelming interest in foreign affairs.

The problem Ford has is that the Democratic party is the majority party and that the voter leans toward it in time of financial crisis. The Republicans have also been in office for eight years in a scandal-racked administration. If there is a third-party candidacy, the votes will probably come from those independents most likely to vote Republican, with the Democrats not hurt at all. If the voters are going "pocketbook" this election, they are not going to waste a vote on anything other than the Democrats.

LOCAL ELECTIONS

Incombency is the single most prominent factor in determining the outcome of local elections. Unless something has happened in the two or four years since the last election, the public will tend to vote for the candidate whom they previously voted into office. This tendency will prevail no matter which office is being sought—governor, senator, representative, state legislator, dog catcher, etc. An incumbent can be defeated only if one or more of the following circumstances is present.

1. The incumbent was not elected, but was appointed to serve out the term of the previous office holder who died or resigned, and this appointed incumbent is of a different political party than the person he replaced.
2. The incumbent was carried into office by the coattails of a candidate running for higher public office, yet is of a different political party than the majority of registered voters in that district or state.
3. The district or state has a relatively even balance between both major political parties and the political party of the challenger is in the ascendancy nationally.

4. A local or national scandal has hit the party of the incumbent.
5. A local scandal has involved the incumbent.
6. The incumbent won his first term by a narrow margin in a year when his party captured the presidency or greatly increased its numbers of voters in local elections.
7. The incumbent is running against the person he replaced by a narrow margin in the last election and the challenger's party is enjoying a resurgence of support nationally or locally.

These circumstances are limited to partisan elections because nonpartisan elections are a bit easier to handicap. The incumbent will win unless a scandal has hit him while in office. Between two nonincumbents, pay close attention to the final pre-election polls. If the margin is fairly close, bet the candidate who has the greatest momentum. Otherwise, just bet the leading candidate if his margin is six percentage points or more in the poll (polls generally allow for a 3 percent margin of error; bettors should take this into account and demand an additional 3 percent edge).

In the partisan elections, the only incumbents who will lose in the general elections are those whose party affiliations ran counter to the general affiliation or current identification of the majority of voters in his district or state. If an officeholder just barely made it last time at a time when he had all the advantages, he will lose if in this election the voters are likely to favor the opposite party.

In general, bet the incumbent unless the aforementioned circumstance prevails.

GLOSSARY

Aces up—A poker hand comprised of two pairs of cards, the higher being a pair of aces.

Across the Board—Betting win, place, and show on one animal.

Allowance race—A race in which the conditions limit entries to horses of fairly equal ability, based on earnings and number or types of wins.

Ante—Chips or cash put in a poker pot before the cards are dealt.

Back line—The section of the craps layout where don't-pass bets are made.

Back-to-back—A pair in stud poker made up of the hole (unexposed) card and the first face-up card; also called being wired.

Bank craps—Casino craps.

Bear in—To run toward the inside of the track rather than straight; applies to horse or dog races.

Bearing out—To drift toward the outside of a race track.

Bet the pot—To make a poker bet equal to the size of the pot.

Bit—metal bar in a horse's mouth attached to the reins.

Blackjack—An ace and a face card or ten on the first two cards dealt; a natural.

Blinkers—Blinders that limit a horse's vision to make it concentrate in a race.

Bluff—To attempt to force other poker players out of the game by convincing them that your losing hand is a sure winner.

Bookmaker—Your friendly neighborhood taker of illegal bets.

Break—The beginning of a race; in harness racing, to shift from a pace or trot into a run.

Bust—A poker hand that can drive you to drink; in black-jack, to exceed twenty-one.

Calk—A cleated horseshoe for mud or grass courses.

Call—To meet a poker bet by putting in the pot the same amount as the previous bet; to bid, pass, or declare.

Card Mechanic—One who uses card skills to cheat.

Cesta—A scoop-like device tied on the wrists of jai alai players in which the ball is caught and then thrown.

Chalk—The favorite in a race.

Check—To pass, in poker, when it is the player's turn to bet.

Claiming race—A race in which horses can be purchased at a set price.

Class—The relative value of a horse or dog based on the size of the purses for which it competes.

Colt—An unaltered male horse four years old and under.

Column bet—In roulette, a bet on twelve vertical numbers of the layout that pays off at odds of 2-1.

Come or don't-come line—Even odds bet after the come-out that the shooter will either hit or miss on the come point.

Come-out—Crap shooter's first roll.

Crap out—To roll a two, three, or twelve on the initial craps roll.

Craps—A dice game; rolling a losing two, three or twelve on the initial craps roll.

Croupier—A casino employee who operates the roulette wheel.

Daily double—A parimutuel bet in which the player buys one ticket stipulating the winners of the first two races.

Dead heat—A tie between two or more finishers in a race.

Double down—A blackjack player's option to double the bet after receiving first two cards.

Early foot—The tendency for horse to start quickly.

Exacta—A parimutuel wager in which the bettor tries to pick the first two finishers of a race, in exact order.

Exotic bets—Any betting other than straight win, place, or show; includes triples, exactas, daily doubles, etc.

Field—A bet in craps that one of several numbers will be rolled next on the dice; all the entrants in a race; a group of lightly regarded horses grouped as a single betting entry.

Filly—A female horse four years old and under.

Flat—The regular dirt racing surface, as opposed to steeplechase or grass courses.

Flush—A poker hand of five cards in one suit (clubs, diamonds, hearts, or spades), not necessarily in sequence.

Fold—To drop out of a poker hand.

Fractions—The speed of a horse clocked at quarter-mile intervals.

Fronton—A jai alai court.

Front-runner—An animal that tends to run in front of the field.

Full house—A poker hand with three of a kind and a pair.

Furlong—One-eighth of a mile.

Gait—The walk, trot, or gallop; the pace of a harness horse.

Gate—The starting gate in a race.

Gin—A winning gin rummy hand of matched sets and sequences with no odd cards.

Good track—A slightly muddy track, usually less speedy.

Grass—A turf race course.

Handicap—A race in which different weights are assigned to horses to equalize their chances of winning; to predict the outcome of a race or sports contest by comparing the past records of the participants.

Handle—The total amount bet on one race or one day or other period.

Hardway bet—A bet that four, six, eight, or ten in craps will be rolled in duplicate numbers before the shooter rolls seven or another combination of the number. Two two's makes four the hardway, etc.

High roller—A big bettor.

Hit—To draw another card in blackjack.

Hole card—The unexposed card or cards in blackjack and stud poker.

Honest pace—A race in which no horse steals a race by taking a prohibitive lead and holding on.

Hopples—The hobbling equipment used on harness horses to keep them from breaking into a run.

House—The casino or game operator.

House advantage—The difference between true odds and payoffs by the gambling operation.

In the money—A parimutuel entry that finishes within the first three.

Insurance bet—An optional blackjack bet that the dealer holds a blackjack when his or her face up card is an ace.

Jackpots—A poker variation in which a pair of jacks or better is required to open the betting.

Kitty—A percentage taken out of the pot to pay expenses.

Knock—To end gin rummy play by laying down your hand before the gin game is over in an attempt to win on points.

Length—Eight or nine feet, the length of a horse.

Linemaker—A person in Las Vegas who makes up the odds or line for sporting events; also called odds maker.

Low hand—The worst hand, winning hand in low-ball poker.

Maiden—A horse that has never won a race; a race for nonwinners.

Mare—A female horse five years old or more.

Misdeal—An irregularity requiring a new shuffle and deal.

Morning line—The forecast of likely odds.

Mudder—A horse that runs well on muddy or wet tracks.

Muddy track—A track that is soft and holding. It is usually slow.

Natural—An ace and a ten or face card in blackjack. In poker, a good hand without a wild card. In craps, rolling a winning seven or eleven on the initial throw.

Odds board—A tote board on which current parimutuel odds are listed.

Odds on—Odds of less than even money or 1-1.

Oddsmaker—See linemaker.

Off track—A racing surface that is other than fast; betting away from the track.

One-run horse—An animal that uses all its energy in one burst of speed.

Open craps—A banking dice game also known as money craps. It is not played at regular casinos.

Overlay—Any bet in which the promised payoff exceeds the chance of winning.

Pacer—The harness horse that runs with hopples on its legs; a gait in which the front and rear leg on one side move forward simultaneously, then the front and rear leg on the other side move.

Paddock—A place where horses are paraded and saddled up before a race.

Parimutuels—A system developed by a Frenchman (originally called Paris mutuels) in which the winning bettors receive the money wagered on a race or match after the house percentage is deducted.

Pass—To decide not to make a bet in poker; in craps, a winning decision for the shooter.

Pass or don't pass—A bet with or against the shooter on the come-out (an even odds bet).

Pelota—A jai alai ball.

Perfecta—An exacta race.

Place—To win second place in a parimutuel bet; in bank craps a right or wrong point bet.

Plater—A claiming horse, cheap animal.

Point—Any number or total in a gambling game on which a wager can be placed. The numbers four, five, six, eight, nine, and ten are possible point numbers in craps; they must be repeated before the roll of seven.

Point spread—The estimated point difference between two football or basketball teams.

Policy—The numbers game.

Pot—A total of chips or money at stake in a betting game.

Pricemake—To determine if a horse or other betting proposition is worth the money at the odds given.

Pricemaker—A track official who assigns odds to horses or dogs in a race; a newspaper or racing sheet writer who tries to select probable winners and probable closing odds.

Proposition bet—A bet in any game not covered by the rules; a bet to settle any difference of opinion.

Punter—A bettor.

Quarterhorse—A speedy western breed used on ranches and for racing short distances.

Quiniela—A bet on the first two finishers of a race or match, in either order.

Racing secretary—The official who assigns conditions of horse races and usually sets weights for handicap races.

Raise—To put more poker chips in the pot than previous bettors.

Route—A distance race.

Rundown—A horse that scrapes its heels on the track while racing; a heel bandage for a horse.

Scratch—To withdraw a horse from a race.

See—To match the previous bet in poker.

Shoe board—A sign showing type of shoes horses are wearing in a race.

Show—The third place in a parimutuel race or match.

Showdown—The point at which cards are shown at the

end of a poker game.

Sloppy track—A track covered with puddles but not yet muddy.

Slow track—A track that is wetter than good, but not as heavy as muddy.

Smart money—Bets made by insiders, professionals.

Sprint—A short race, usually seven furlongs or less.

Stakes—A race in which the purse is made up of nomination, entry and starting fees plus other money added by the track.

Stiff—To prevent a horse from winning by a deliberately poor ride or drugging; a poor horse; a poor hand in blackjack.

Straight—A poker hand of five cards in a sequence of different suits.

Table stakes—A method of placing a maximum betting limit on wagers in poker.

Takeout—The percentage that the track takes out of wagers.

Tote board—The odds board.

Triple—An exotic bet in which first three finishers must be picked in exact order.

Trotters—A harness horse that races without hopples and moves one front leg and the opposite rear leg in unison.

Turf—A grassy thoroughbred race course.

Underknock—To show a hand in gin rummy that has the same or fewer points in unmatched cards than the player who has knocked.

Underlay—To bet at odds below the chances of winning.

Wild card—A certain card designated by the dealer in poker that can be any value or suit the player prefers.

Wired—A player who has a pair back-to-back in stud poker.

Workout—The morning practice run for thoroughbreds.

APPENDIX A

Parimutuel Payoffs

Odds to $1	Payoffs on standard $2 ticket
1-20	$ 2.10
1-10	2.20
1-5	2.40
2-5	2.80
1-2	3.00
3-5	3.20
4-5	3.60
even	4.00
6-5	4.40
7-5	4.80
3-2	5.00
8-5	5.20
9-5	5.60
2-1	6.00
5-2	7.00
3-1	8.00
7-2	9.00
4-1	10.00
9-2	11.00
5-1	12.00
6-1	14.00
7-1	16.00
8-1	18.00
9-1	20.00
10-1	22.00
20-1	42.00
50-1	102.00

Note: Many tracks will have a minimum win payoff of $2.20; odds to $1 will not go below 1-10.

APPENDIX B

How Betting Against the Shooter Can Result in Ultimate Victory in Private Craps

110 X 36 = 3960 rolls

			Times thrown	*Winners*
Natural 7	6:36	=	66	660
Natural 11	2:36	=	220	220
Craps 2	1:36	=	110	—
Craps 3	2:36	=	220	—
Craps 12	1:36	=	110	—
Point 4	3 chances to make 6 chances to lose or 1 win for 2 losses			
	3:36	=	330	110
Point 5	4 chances to hit—6 chances to lose			
	4:36	=	440	176
Point 6	5 chances to hit—6 chances to lose			
	5:36	=	550	230
Point 8	5 chances to hit—6 chances to lose			
	5:36	=	550	250
Point 9	4 chances to hit—6 chances to lose			
	4:36	=	440	176
Point 10	3 chances to hit—6 chances to lose			
	3:36	=	330	110
			3,960	1,952

Note: There are 3,960 rolls, 1,952 winners, and 2,008 losers. This means there are 56 less winners than losers, which gives a 1.41 percent advantage betting against the shooter.

HOW TO READ "TOMORROW'S TROTS"

The number to the left of the horse's name is the morning line or probable odds. The initials immediately following the horse's name represent color and sex, figures denote age. The names following are the horse's sire, dam, dam's sire and trainer in that order. In parentheses under the horse's name is the horse's lifetime earnings up to Jan. 1 of the current year. Also, lifetime win record, age when made and size of track, except half-mile track, through Dec. 31 of previous year. Then come the driver's name, weight and his colors. Alongside of that are the horse's last year's best winning time and track where made. Then his number of starts, how many times he finished first, second or third and his money winnings. Beneath the horse's earnings are records of his eight most recent races. They read from botton to top, therefore the top is the horse's latest race.

The date of the race is followed by the name of the track. All tracks are half-mile unless followed by the figure (1) which means that it is a mile track; or (¾) which is a three-quarter mile track, etc. Then is noted the condition of the track on the day of the race and the type of the race. Where money figures follow track condition it denotes price of horse in claiming race. Race distance time of leading horse at ¼, ½ and ¾ follow, then comes the winner's time. The figures that follow in order show the post positions of the horse, his position at the ¼, ½, ¾, stretch with lengths behind except for the leading horse whose number denotes lengths ahead; and finish with beaten lengths. If he was the winner it shows how far he was ahead of the second horse and the loser's show how far they were behind the winning horse. The next figure shows the horse's actual time in that race. Wherever a small "°" appears after the calls, it denotes that the horse raced on the outside at least one quarter of a mile. In some instances these figures won't appear because the track at which the horse raced did not have its races charted. Then follows the closing odds to the dollar, the horse's driver, and order of finish, giving the names of the first three horses.

In all races of ¾ mile or less, the fractional times will be carried for the ¼, ½, and the time of race. In races of 1 1/16 and 1⅛ miles the times will be carried for ½, ¾, Mile, and finish. In 1¼ mile races the times will be at ½, Mile, 1¼ and finish. Positions of the horses will correspond with the times in 1⅛ and 1¼ mile races.

ABBREVIATIONS AND SYMBOLS

HORSES COLOR AND SEX

b g—bay gelding
blk c—black colt
br m—brown mare
ch h—chestnut horse
gr f—grey filly
ro—roan

TRACK SIZE

(⅝)—⅝ mile track
(¾)—¾ mile track
(1)—one mile track

TRACK CONDITIONS

ft—fast
gd—good
sy—sloppy
sl—slow
hy—heavy
my—muddy

TYPE OF RACE

Cd 2000—Conditioned & Purse
Stk—Stake
clm 3000—$3,000 claiming race (act. value on this horse)
nw 3000 (non-winners $3,000; etc); Opt—optional claimer
cl—classified
ec—early closer
lc—late closer
qua—qualifying
dr qua—Driver Qualifying
mdn—maiden
Opn—Open
hcp—Handicap
Inv—Invitational
tp—Trot and Pace
alw—Allowance Races
Pref—Preferred

RACING INFORMATION

x—Break
i—Interference
ix—Interference Break
ex—Equipment Break
°—Parked Out
°°—Parked Out 3 Wide
°9—Started Nine Abreast
ᵒ—Blocked in stretch
wkt—Workout
be—Broken Equipment
(P)—Provisional Driver
‡—Free-legged Pacer
‡—Hobbled Trotter
†—Half Hopples
m—One Mile
Z—Horse Claimed
(NY) —N.Y. State Bred

WAGERING INFORMATION

f—mutuel field
e—entry
*—favorite
NB—No Betting
NR—Not Reported
DNF—Did Not Finish

FINISH INFORMATION

ns—nose
hd—head
nk—neck
dh—dead heat
dis—distanced
dq—disqualified

MORNING LINE / Free Legged / Horse's Name / Lifetime Win Record / Age When Made / Size of Track / Horse's Color / Sex / Age / Sire / Dam / Dam's Sire / Best Win Time This Year / Name of Trainer / Name of Stable

6	‡PAPPYS JOY (NY)					blk h, 7, by Flow Up, Jenny VI by Jay Guy											(Tr.-J. Jones)		(St.-R. Jones)
						Owner-Gay Stables, New York, N.Y.									YR 2:03:1	1975	26 5 6 3		24,162.
	($36,243) 3, 2:02:4 (1)					(P) ABE SMITH (150)					Green-White				Lex(1) 2:02:4	1974	3 1 0 0		1,080.
	6-30 YR‡	ft B-1	3500	m	29:4	1:01:3	1:34	2:04:1	7	3°	1	1	3/½	4/1¾ dq	2:04:3	8.10(Cllhn)	CloudyBay,	AdiosPetr,	FishCounsl
	6-24 YR‡	ft B-1	3500	m	29:3	1:01	1:32	2:02:4	6	x8x	8	8°	8/4¼	4/2¾	2:03:2	8.00(Cllhn)	GoodShot,	StormyDream,	KeyCity

Date of Race / Track Raced On / Track Condition / Age, Type of Race, Purse / Distance of Race / Time at ¼ / Time at ½ / Time at ¾ / Time of Winner / Post Position / Position at ¼ / Position at ½ / Position at ¾ / Stretch Position and Lengths / Finish Position and Lengths / Actual Time / Odds to 1.00 / Best Win Time Last Year / Driver / Name of Winner / Second Horse / Third Horse

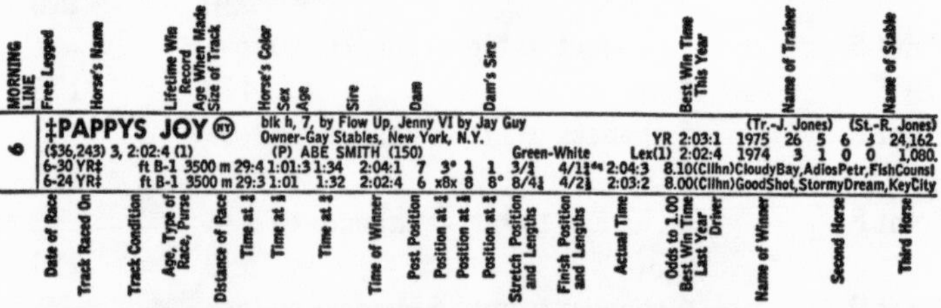

TRACK ABBREVIATIONS AND COMPARATIVE SPEED RATING

Track	Abbrev	Time
Atlantic City Raceway (⅝ mile)	AC(⅝)	2:03:2
Aurora Downs	Aur	2:07
Balmoral Park	BlmP	2:06
Batavia	Btva.	2:05:1
Bay Meadows (one mile)	B.M.(1)	2:04
Blue Bonnets (⅝ mile)	B.B.(⅝)	2:03:1
Brandywine (⅝ mile)	Brd(⅝)	2:02:3
Buffalo	B.R.	2:05:1
Cahokia Downs (¾)	Cka(¾)	2:04:1
Connaught Park	Conn	2:06:1
Delaware	Dela.	2:04:3
Detroit (Wolverine) (1) 1970	Det.(1)	2:03:2
Dover Downs (⅝ mile)	D.D.(⅝)	2:04:2
DuQuoin (one mile)	DuQ.(1)	2:01:3
East Moline Downs (⅝)	EMDn(⅝)	
Fairmont Park (one mile)	F.P.(1)	
Foxboro(⅝)	Fox(⅝)	2:03:4
Freehold	Fhld	2:04:3
Frontenac Downs (⅝ mile)	FD(⅝)	2:04:1
Garden City, Can. (⅝ mile)	GdnC(⅝)	2:04:3
Georgetown Raceway	GR	2:05:2
Goshen	Gosh.	2:05
Green Mountain (11/16 mile)	G.M.(11/16)	2:04:3
Greenwood, Can. (⅝ mile)	GrR(⅝)	2:04
Hamilton	H.R.	2:06:2
Harrington	Harr.	2:05:2
Hawthorne (one mile)	Haw(1)	2:03:4
Hazel Park (⅝ mile)	H.P.(⅝)	2:04
Hinsdale	Hin.	2:06:1
Hollywood Park (one mile)	Hol.(1)	2:01:4
Indianapolis (one mile)	Ind.(1)	2:01:4
Jackson	Jack.	2:07
Latonia, Ky. (one mile)	Lat(1)	2:04:3
Laurel (⅝ mile)	Lau(⅝)	2:03:1
Lebanon	Leb	2:06:2
Lewiston	Lew	2:05:2
Lexington (one mile)	Lex.(1)	2:01:2
Liberty Bell (⅝ mile)	L.B.(⅝)	2:02:3
Lincoln Downs (13/16)	L.D.(13/16)	2:03:3
Los Alamitos (⅝ mile)	LAl(⅝)	2:03:4
Louisville Downs	LouD	2:05:2
Maywood	May.	2:05
Mohawk, Can. (⅝ mile)	Mhk(⅝)	2:04:1
Monticello	M.R.	2:05:1
Midwest (Audubon)	Mid	2:05:2
Northfield	Nfld.	2:05
Northville Downs	Nor.	2:05
Ocean Downs	O.D.	2:04:3
Pocono Downs (⅝ mile)	PcD(⅝)	2:03:1
Pompano Park (⅝ mile)	P.Pk(⅝)	2:03:2
Rcway Prk (Toledo) (⅝)	R.Pk.(⅝)	
Richelieu Park	Rich.	2:04:4
Rideau Carlton (⅝)	RidC(⅝)	2:04:1
Rockingham	Rock.	2:05:4
Roosevelt	R.R.	2:04:1
Rosecroft	RcR.	2:04:1
Saratoga	Stga.	2:03:2
Scarborough	Scar	
Scioto Downs (⅝ mile)	Sc.D.(⅝)	2:02:3
Seminole Pk. (¾) Orlando, Fla.	Sem(¾)	
Sportsman's Park (⅝ mile)	Spk.(⅝)	2:03:4
Springfield (one mile)	Spr.(1)	2:01:3
Syracuse (one mile)	Syr(1)	No Rating
The Meadows, Pa. (⅝)	Mdws(⅝)	2:03:1
Vernon Downs (¾ mile)	V.D.(¾)	2:02
Washington Pk. (one mile)	Was(1)	2:03:1
Wheeling Downs	W.D.	2:05:3
Windsor Raceway (⅝ mile)	W.R.(⅝)	2:03:1
Yonkers	Y.R.	2:04